Contents

27023

Introduction

Mental Illness is Volume 275 in the **ISSUES** series. The aim of the series is to offer current, diverse information about important issues in our world, from a UK perspective.

ABOUT MENTAL ILLNESS

Mental illness and mental health problems are often taboo subjects. To better understand them, however, it is important to open a dialogue that addresses these topics honestly and sensitively. This book looks at mental illness, mental health and the many associated issues. It considers how many people have experienced mental health problems, how we can stay mentally 'healthy', how much mental illness costs the NHS and what affects our mental health the most.

OUR SOURCES

Titles in the **ISSUES** series are designed to function as educational resource books, providing a balanced overview of a specific subject.

The information in our books is comprised of facts, articles and opinions from many different sources, including:

⇨ Newspaper reports and opinion pieces

⇨ Website factsheets

⇨ Magazine and journal articles

⇨ Statistics and surveys

⇨ Government reports

⇨ Literature from special interest groups.

A NOTE ON CRITICAL EVALUATION

Because the information reprinted here is from a number of different sources, readers should bear in mind the origin of the text and whether the source is likely to have a particular bias when presenting information (or when conducting their research). It is hoped that, as you read about the many aspects of the issues explored in this book, you will critically evaluate the information presented.

It is important that you decide whether you are being presented with facts or opinions. Does the writer give a biased or unbiased report? If an opinion is being expressed, do you agree with the writer? Is there potential bias to the 'facts' or statistics behind an article?

ASSIGNMENTS

In the back of this book, you will find a selection of assignments designed to help you engage with the articles you have been reading and to explore your own opinions. Some tasks will take longer than others and there is a mixture of design, writing and research-based activities that you can complete alone or in a group.

FURTHER RESEARCH

At the end of each article we have listed its source and a website that you can visit if you would like to conduct your own research. Please remember to critically evaluate any sources that you consult and consider whether the information you are viewing is accurate and unbiased.

Useful weblinks

www.alzheimers.org.uk

www.babcp.com

www.bham.ac.uk

www.bupa.co.uk

www.channel4.com

www.communitycare.co.uk

www.cqc.org.uk Care Quality Commission

www.cypnow.co.uk Children & Young People Now

wtwww.fph.org.uk Faculty of Public Health

www.fullfact.org

www.healthcare-today.co.uk

www.healthyworkinglives.com

www.justiceinspectorates.gov.uk

www.kcl.ac.uk Kings College London

www.mentalhealthy.co.uk

www.mind.org.uk

www.nhs.uk

www.nhsconfed.org/MHN

www.rethink.org

www.spunout.ie

www.theconversation.com

www.time-to-change.com

www.youngminds.org.uk

Independence Educational Publishers

First published by Independence Educational Publishers

The Studio, High Green

Great Shelford

Cambridge CB22 5EG

England

© Independence 2015

Photocopy licence

The material in this book is protected by copyright. However, the
purchaser is free to make multiple copies of particular articles for instructional
purposes for immediate use within the purchasing institution.
Making copies of the entire book is not permitted.

British Library Cataloguing in Publication Data

Mental illness. -- (Issues ; 275)

1. Mental illness. 2. Mentally ill.

I. Series II. Acred, Cara editor.

362.2-dc23

ISBN-13: 9781861687036

Printed in Great Britain

Zenith Print Group

What is mental health and mental illness?

We often talk about mental health and mental illness. But what do we mean by mental health and emotional well-being and what can you do to look after your own mental health?

What do we mean by mental health?

There is often a lot of confusion about what we mean when we talk about mental health. Many people immediately start thinking about mental health problems or mental illness – but this is only one part of the picture...

Everyone has 'mental health' and this can be thought of in terms of:

⇨ how we feel about ourselves and the people around us

⇨ our ability to make and keep friends and relationships

⇨ our ability to learn from others and to develop psychologically and emotionally.

Being mentally healthy is also about having the strength to overcome the difficulties and challenges we can all face at times in our lives – to have confidence and self-esteem, to be able to take decisions and to believe in ourselves.

Dealing with life's ups and downs

Having said that we all have mental health, it's also important to understand when you might need to get some help or support with how you are feeling – or to know when perhaps you may be experiencing a more serious problem.

It is quite normal to sometimes feel worried, anxious or upset when things don't go as you hope – everyone faces pressure in their lives at certain times and these can include:

⇨ exams

⇨ work and getting a job

⇨ growing up and becoming more independent from your family

⇨ making up (and breaking up) with friends.

You can find more information to help if you are feeling stressed or under pressure from any of these things in the mental health tips on the rethink website.

Knowing when to get help and advice

What to look out for

If someone is experiencing worries, anxieties and difficult feelings to the extent that they are seriously interfering with their everyday life, for instance:

⇨ being able to study and go to school

⇨ being able to eat or sleep as they normally do

⇨ to go out with their friends or take part in their favourite hobby

...and these feelings are becoming persistent – that is, lasting for a few weeks or more – then it might be that they have a mental health problem or disorder and need to get some advice and help.

Mental health problems affect many more young people than you probably realise

Around one in ten of all young people may experience a mental health problem or disorder where they may need help from a mental health specialist.

It's important to get help early. Mental health conditions can be treated and getting help early can prevent difficulties from getting more serious.

There are many different types of mental health problems and they affect young people differently and last for different lengths of time.

⇨ The above information is reprinted with kind permission from Rethink Mental Illness. Please visit www. rethink.org for further information.

Television dramas help public better understand mental health issues, say experts

Television storylines in shows such as *Coronation Street*, *EastEnders* and *Homeland* help viewers understand mental health issues better, according to new research.

Academics studied TV dramas, including soaps, and found that the way mental health issues are portrayed on screen is becoming more realistic and is more likely to encourage people to seek help for their own problems.

The report, by campaign group Time to Change, found mental health issues featuring more often in plot lines than five years ago but warned there were still some 'simplistic portrayals' and misinformation.

More than 2,000 viewers were questioned as part of the research with more than half (54%) saying that seeing a well-known character on screen portrayed as having a mental health problem improved their understanding of what it involved.

Almost half (48%) said it helped change their opinion about who can develop such problems and nearly a third (31%) said they had discussed storylines with friends or family.

Stuart Blackburn, the producer of *Coronation Street* which is about to feature a story where one if its best-known characters, Steve McDonald, is diagnosed with depression, said it was a 'challenge' for the show.

He said: 'A particular challenge we faced with Steve and his depression is the audience's fear that the Steve they loved is gone for good.

'What viewers love about him primarily is the comedy – he's affable, hapless Steve, the bloke next door. But I've told the writers his DNA hasn't changed.

'His head might be taking a battering at the moment, but he still has the same wit, still has good days and bad days. And you can't rush the story.

'We've got to find a way to tell the truth about this, warts and all, and entertain the audience. You hope a show like Corrie can genuinely make a difference to tens if not hundreds of thousands of people, who'll be watching with different eyes or thinking "Maybe I should go to the doctor" – but we won't get through to them if they're turning off.'

Sue Baker, director of Time to Change, said television had the 'ability to shape and form public opinion'.

She said: 'It's important that some of the country's best loved soaps and drama series are taking on mental health storylines, doing them accurately, not fuelling stigma, and helping improve understanding.'

11 November 2014

⇨ The above information is reprinted with kind permission from Press Association. Please visit www.pressassociation.com for further information.

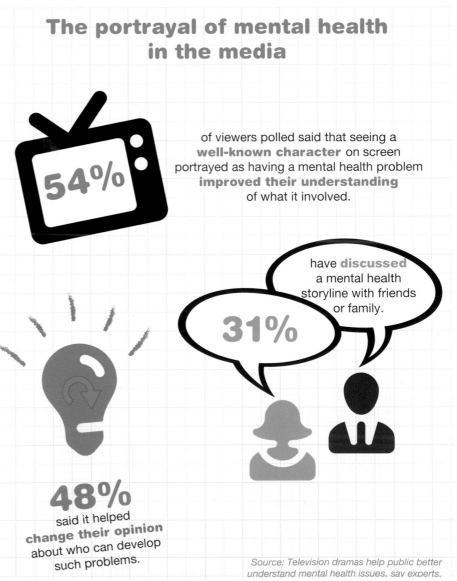

The portrayal of mental health in the media

54% of viewers polled said that seeing a **well-known character** on screen portrayed as having a mental health problem **improved their understanding** of what it involved.

31% have **discussed** a mental health storyline with friends or family.

48% said it helped **change their opinion** about who can develop such problems.

Source: Television dramas help public better understand mental health issues, say experts.

Five new mental disorders you could have under *DSM-5*

THE CONVERSATION

An article from The Conversation.

Written by Christopher Fairburn (Professor of Psychiatry at University of Oxford), Christopher Lane (Professor of English at Northwestern University), David Mataix-Cols (Professor and Honorary Consultant Clinical Psychologist at King's College London), Jie Tian (Professor of Automation at Chinese Academy of Sciences), Jon Grant (Professor of Psychiatry and Behavioral Neuroscience at University of Chicago) and Karen M. von Deneen (Associate Professor at Xidian University)

Since it was first published in 1952, the *DSM* has been the diagnostic bible for many psychiatrists. Each time the manual is updated, new conditions are introduced, often amid much controversy. *DSM-5*, the latest edition published on Saturday, is one of the most controversial yet.

Many conditions we're now familiar with were codified in the *DSM*, including body dismorphic disorder, schizophrenia and bipolar disorder.

Inclusions and removals can be hugely controversial. Autism is in the manual, for example, but Asperger's isn't. Homosexuality was only removed in 1974.

Below, five experts explain some of the most noteworthy new additions, and why they've been included.

Hoarding disorder

David Mataix-Cols: Most children have collections at some point and approximately 30% of British adults define themselves as collectors.

This is a pleasurable, highly social and benign activity, which contrasts with another disabling form of object accumulation: hoarding disorder.

The symptoms include persistent difficulty in discarding possessions due to a strong perceived need to save items and distress in discarding them. This results in the accumulation of a large number of possessions that fill up and clutter key living areas of the home, to the extent that their intended use is no longer possible.

Symptoms are often accompanied by excessive acquiring, buying or even stealing of items that are not needed or for which there is no available space.

Using *DSM-5*, hoarding disorder can only be diagnosed once other mental disorders have been ruled out.

With a prevalence of at least 1.5% of the UK population, the disorder is associated with substantial functional disability, family conflict, social isolation, risk of falls and fires, evictions and homelessness.

Binge eating disorder

Christopher Fairburn: The inclusion of binge eating disorder in the *DSM-5* was expected and uncontroversial for the deciding committee. It's already listed as a provisional diagnosis in the *DSM-4*.

The disorder is characterised by recurrent over-eating episodes and a sense of loss of control at the time. Sufferers don't have the extreme dieting, vomiting and laxative misuse seen in people who have bulimia. It is the loss of control over eating that is the distressing feature of binge eating disorder, or BED.

BED is very different from anorexia nervosa and bulimia nervosa. These disorders are largely confined to young women and they share many features including highly distinctive concerns about shape and weight and extreme weight control behaviour, such as dieting. None of this is present in people with BED.

BED is typically seen among those who are middle aged. Men make up about a third of cases. The disorders also differ in their response to treatment. Unlike anorexia and bulimia, people who suffer from binge eating disorder respond well to a variety of treatments.

Skin picking disorder

Jon Grant: Skin picking has been documented in medical literature since the 19th century but only now has it been recognised in the *DSM-5*.

Skin picking disorder affects around 2–5% of people in the US. It is not simply a harmless habit nor merely

I HAD THIS OBSESSION ABOUT COLLECTING BARBIES. WOULD YOU BELIEVE THAT MY WIFE RAN OFF WITH A MAN CALLED KEN?!

a symptom of another disorder. Skin picking may result in significant tissue damage and often leads to medical complications such as local infections and septicaemia.

Sufferers of the disorder are diagnosed according to five criteria, including recurrent skin picking that causes skin lesions; repeated attempts to cut down or stop; and that the skin picking causes significant distress or problems in social situations, work, or other important areas in life.

Skin picking also can't exist due to the physical effects of a substance or a medical condition, or be linked to another mental disorder – for example, because someone has body dysmorphic disorder. These criteria separate people who only pick their skin occasionally.

Data from multiple researchers around the world consistently show that skin-picking disorder has distinct characteristics, important neurobiological links, and documented responsiveness to treatments – both Cognitive Behaviour Therapy and medication can work.

Somatic symptom disorder

Christopher Lane: Somatic comes from the Greek word for 'of the body', the focus of the disorder. *DSM*'s earlier family of medically unexplained ailments grouped together problems as different as hypochondria and body dysmorphia and so the American Psychiatric Association proposed somatic symptom disorder.

It's a new, stand-alone disorder for people who experience a 'disproportionate' sense of anxiety about their health and at least one physical symptom, such as a persistent headache.

People can be diagnosed with the new disorder if their physical symptoms are distressing and/or disruptive to their daily life for at least six months, and they also have one of the following: disproportionate thoughts about the seriousness of their symptoms; or a high level of anxiety about their symptoms or health; or they devote excessive time and energy to their symptoms or health concerns.

There have been concerns because the threshold of 'disproportionate' and 'excessive' is difficult to quantify and the disorder could be used as a catch-all for many people.

Internet addiction

Karen M. von Deneen, Jie Tian: While not yet officially codified within a psychopathological framework, Internet addiction is growing in prevalence and has attracted the attention of psychiatrists, educators and the public.

Internet addiction is a newly identified condition associated with loss of control over Internet use. It leads to negative psychosocial and physical results, such as impairment of academic failure, social deficits, criminal activities and even death. This consists of three main subtypes: excessive gaming, sexual preoccupations, and email/text messaging.

The *DSM-5* now includes a newly-created category of behavioural addictions, in which gambling will be the sole disorder. Internet addiction was considered for this category, but work group members decided there was insufficient research data to do so, so they recommended it be included in the manual's appendix instead, with the goal of encouraging additional study.

Present treatment has included electric shock therapy and Internet rehab, but these have not been satisfactory. More research needs to be done to understand the underlying mechanisms of this addiction.

20 May 2013

⇨ The above information is reprinted with kind permission from The Conversation Trust (UK). Please visit www. theconversation.com further information.

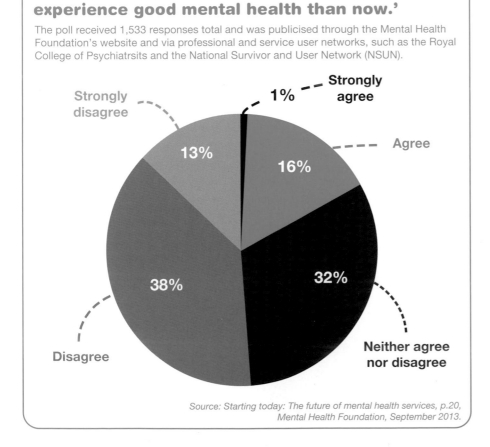

'In 20 years' time, more people in later life will experience good mental health than now.'

The poll received 1,533 responses total and was publicised through the Mental Health Foundation's website and via professional and service user networks, such as the Royal College of Psychiatrsits and the National Survivor and User Network (NSUN).

- Strongly disagree – 13%
- Strongly agree – 1%
- Agree – 16%
- Neither agree nor disagree – 32%
- Disagree – 38%

Source: Starting today: The future of mental health services, p.20, Mental Health Foundation, September 2013.

Mental health statistics, facts and myths

These key facts and statistics about mental health problems can help to challenge the myths that can contribute to the stigma that many people still face.

It's so important that we challenge these myths so we can understand the real facts about what mental health problems are and how they can affect people.

Mental health myths and facts

Myth: Mental health problems are very rare.

Fact: One in four people will experience a mental health problem in any given year.

Myth: People with mental illness aren't able to work.

Fact: We probably all work with someone experiencing a mental health problem.

Myth: Young people just go through ups and downs as part of puberty, it's nothing.

Fact: One in ten young people will experience a mental health problem.

Myth: People with mental health illnesses are usually violent and unpredictable.

Fact: People with a mental illness are more likely to be a victim of violence.

Myth: People with mental health problems don't experience discrimination

Fact: Nine out of ten people with mental health problems experience stigma and discrimination.

Myth: It's easy for young people to talk to friends about their feelings.

Fact: Nearly three in four young people fear the reactions of friends when they talk about their mental health problems.

Statistics about violence and mental illness

The majority of violent crimes and homicides are committed by people who do not have mental health problems.

People with mental health problems are more dangerous to themselves than they are to others: 90 per cent of people who die through suicide in the UK are experiencing mental distress

In 2009, the total population in England and Wales aged 16 or over was just over 43 million. It is estimated that about one in six of the adult population will have a significant mental health problem at any one time, (more than seven million people). Given this number and the 50–70 cases of homicide a year involving people known to have a mental health problem at the time of the murder, clearly the statistics data do not support the sensationalised media coverage about the danger that people with mental health problems present to the community.

Substance abuse appears to play a role: the prevalence of violence is higher among people who have symptoms of substance abuse (discharged psychiatric patients and non-patients).

Read our guidelines for reporting stories featuring violence and mental health problems (http://www.time-to-change.org.uk/news-media/media-advisory-service/help-journalists/violence-mental-health-problems) for more information.

Facts about portrayals of mental health in TV dramas and soaps

Research was carried out around portrayals of mental health in television drama and soaps, this found:

⇨ over a three-month period 74 programmes contained storylines on mental health issues, of these there were 33 instances of violence to others and 53 examples of harm to self

⇨ almost half were sympathetic portrayals, but these often portrayed the characters as tragic victims

⇨ the most commonly referred to condition was depression, which was mentioned 19 times, breakdown was mentioned eight times and bipolar seven

⇨ 63% of references to mental health in TV soaps and drama were 'pejorative, flippant or unsympathetic' terms and included: 'crackpot', 'a sad little psycho', 'basket case', 'where did you get her from?', 'Care in the Community?' and 'he was looney tunes'.

Read our media guidelines (http://www.time-to-change.org.uk/media-centre/media-advisory-service/soaps-dramas) for people working on mental health storylines in TV dramas and soaps.

Other sources of information

Find out more facts and statistics about mental health from:

⇨ Mental Health Foundation

⇨ Mind

⇨ Young Minds

⇨ Suicide facts and figures from the Samaritans.

⇨ The above information is reprinted with kind permission from Time To Change. Please visit www.time-to-change.com further information.

© Mind 2014

Key facts and trends in mental health

2014 update.

The following article is an extract from the third edition of the Mental Health Network factsheet giving an overview of the major trends and challenges facing mental health services.

Investment in services

Real terms decline in funding

The Department of Health's latest surveys of investment in adult and older people's mental health services cover services in England for the 2011/12 financial year. They underline the scale of the financial challenge currently facing mental health services.

The 2011/12 survey found investment in mental health services for adults of working age (aged 18–64) dropped by one per cent in real terms from the previous year. This was the first real terms drop in investment since the survey began in 2001/02. In cash terms, there was an increase of 1.2 per cent in 2011/12, to a total of £6.629 billion.

Investment across the three priority areas (crisis resolution, early intervention and assertive outreach) fell, for the first time, by £29.3 million. Funding for psychological therapies increased by six per cent in real terms compared to 2010/11.

Funding for older people's mental health services was found to be under greater pressure, with a one per cent cash-terms drop from the previous year to £2.830 billion in 2011/12. This represents a decrease in real terms of 3.1 per cent.

There is no national survey data available to cover 2012/13 or 2013/14. The BBC and Community Care published figures in December 2013, based on Freedom of Information request responses from 43 of 51 mental health trusts. Comparing 2011/12 budgets with those for this year, 2013/14, they found a real-terms reduction of 2.36 per cent over the two-year period.

There is currently no comparable national investment survey for child and adolescent mental health services (CAMHS). YoungMinds' most recent survey found 67 per cent of councils had reduced CAMHS funding between 2010 and 2013. Regional cuts in spending were as high as 12 per cent in the North East and 13 per cent in East of England.

Trends in morbidity

The 2007 adult psychiatric morbidity survey found that the proportion of the English population aged between 16 and 64 meeting the criteria for one common mental disorder increased from 15.5 per cent in 1993 to 17.6 per cent in 2007. 24 per cent of those with a common mental disorder were receiving treatment.

Household income correlates strongly with incidence of common mental health problems. This pattern is more marked amongst men than women. After adjusting for age, men in the lowest household income group were three times more likely to have a common mental disorder than those in the highest income households (23.5 per cent and 8.8 per cent, respectively).

The same survey found that psychotic disorders were experienced by 0.4 per cent of the population in 2007 (0.3 per cent of men and 0.5 per cent of women). The Mental Health Network understands that the adult psychiatric morbidity survey will be repeated in 2014.

Statistics relating to the mental health of children and young people are highlighted later in this article (see 'Children and young people').

Suicide rates

The latest report from the National Confidential Inquiry into Suicide and Homicide by People with Mental Illness (NCI) found that suicide by mental health patients in England had risen, with 1,333 deaths in 2011. A change to the coding of causes of death has contributed to this figure and changes to the Mental Health Minimum Dataset

(MHMDS) method make comparisons with earlier years difficult. However, it is likely that this represents a true rise in patient suicide, following a previous fall. The NCI speculates that the rise 'probably reflects the rise in suicide in the general population, which has been attributed to current economic difficulties.'

Homicide rates

Homicide by mental health patients has fallen since a peak in 2006. Figures for the most recent confirmed years, 2009/10, are the lowest since the NCI began data collection in 1997, with 33 cases reported in 2010 in England. The NCI says that delays in the criminal justice system and in data processing may have contributed, but 'it is likely that this is a true fall in patient homicide.'

Service activity

There were nearly 1.6 million (1,590,332) people in contact with specialist mental health services in 2012/13.

Of this total, 105,224 service users (6.6 per cent of all service users) spent time in hospital at some point in the year. This is a small increase from 6.3 per cent of all service users in 2011/12. Eight per cent of male service users spent time in hospital, compared with 5.5 per cent of female service users.

During November and December 2013 the Mental Health Network conducted a member survey on activity in crisis services. 20 per cent of our 64 member organisations responded. Whilst the results therefore should be treated with some caution, the vast majority of respondents reported an increase in demand for crisis services in the last 12 months (92 per cent). Over half (55 per cent) of respondents reported there was a 11–20 per cent increase in demand for crisis services.

People in contact with NHS-funded adult specialist mental health services spent over eight million (8,133,764) days in hospital in 2012/13

– an increase of just over 515,000 bed days from 7,618,269 in 2011/12. Over 90 per cent of in-year bed days were in the statutory sector. Whilst not all independent sector providers returned data through the Mental Health Minimum Dataset, there were 789,233 in-year bed days recorded amongst this group of providers.

The Care Quality Commission has highlighted concerns about occupancy levels at mental health inpatient facilities. In 2011/12, 16 per cent of wards visited by Mental Health Act Commissioners had occupancy levels of 100 per cent or more. Around half of wards had an occupancy level of 90 per cent or less.

Outpatient and community services

There were 21,722,314 outpatient and community contacts arranged in 2012/13 – a slight decrease of 0.2 per cent (from 21,774,633 contacts) in 2011/12.

Use of the Mental Health Act and community treatment orders

In the reporting year 2012/13, there were 50,408 detentions under the Mental Health Act. This is four per cent (1,777) greater than during the 2011/12 reporting period.

Of those people who spent time in hospital, 45.6 per cent were subject to the Mental Health Act at some point in 2012/13. Males aged 18 to 35 were most likely (56.1 per cent) to be subject to the Mental Health Act.

The Health & Social Care Information Centre states that amongst statutory NHS providers, the data shows an 8.7 per cent increase in the number of inpatients being subject to the Mental Health Act during the year. This suggests a continuing trend for psychiatric beds to be increasingly occupied by people subject to some form of legal restriction.

Around 42 per cent of inpatients in the White ethnic groups were subject to some form of restriction under the Mental Health Act. Around 70 per cent of inpatients in the Black or Black British ethnic groups were subject to a form of compulsory detention during 2012/13.

On 31 March 2013, there were 5,218 people subject to community treatment orders. This is an increase of ten per cent since the same day of the previous year.

Children and young people

In 2004, the Office for National Statistics estimated that one in ten children and young people between the ages of five and 16 had a clinically diagnosed mental health disorder.

This included four per cent with an emotional disorder (three per cent anxiety disorders and one per cent depression), six per cent with a conduct disorder, two per cent with a hyperkinetic disorder and less than 1 per cent with a less common disorder (including autism, tics and eating disorders). Some children had more than one disorder. There was no statistically significant change in the rates of disorders over the period from the previous survey in 1999.

Between one in 12 and one in 15 children and young people are thought to deliberately self-harm.

Children and adolescents with poor mental health have relatively worse prospects throughout their adult life. For example, young people with mild conduct problems in adolescence are twice as likely to have no educational qualifications in early adulthood. Those with severe conduct problems were up to four times more likely to have been arrested by the police by the age of 30.

Inpatient admissions

There were 3,626 inpatient admissions for child and adolescent psychiatry specialities in 2011/12, compared to 3,136 admissions in the previous year – a 15.6 per cent increase. In 2012/13, total admissions totalled 3,548, with emergency admissions making up 1,574 of the total. The number of admissions is now around double that at the turn of the millennium.

Outpatient attendances

Under the child and adolescent psychiatry speciality there were a total of 240,554 outpatient attendances in 2012/13, compared with 284,674 in 2011/12. First appointment attendances in 2012/13 totalled 38,288, a considerable drop from

50,366 in 2011/12. There were 4,185 first tele-consultation attendances in 2012/13, compared with 3,248 in 2011/12.

Service user experience

More than 13,000 service users responded to the Care Quality Commission's 2013 survey of community mental health services across 58 NHS trusts. Sixty seven per cent of respondents rated their experience between seven and ten out of ten.

78 per cent said they 'definitely' felt listened to carefully. 72 per cent had 'definitely' had their views taken into account by the health or social care worker they had seen most recently.

Of the two-fifths of respondents who had received talking therapies, 89 per cent found it to be helpful, either 'definitely' (52 per cent) or 'to some extent' (37 per cent).

Of those respondents with a physical health condition, 37 per cent would have liked support in connection with their physical health needs but did not receive it.

Service users on the Care Programme Approach (CPA) should be able to access support regarding employment, housing and finance if required. However, 32 per cent reported they had not had support with employment, 28 per cent had not received housing support and 27 per cent had not received help with managing finances.

46 per cent of those on CPA 'definitely' understood the contents of their care plan – two per cent less than in 2012. 58 per cent of the same group confirmed their care plan 'definitely' covers what they should do in a time of crisis – also two per cent down on 2012.

Of those prescribed new medications, 28 per cent said they had not been told of possible side effects and 16 per cent felt they weren't provided with easily understood information about the medicine.

Inequalities

BME service users

The Count Me In censuses, published annually up to 2011 by the Care Quality

Commission, consistently highlighted that rates of admission and detentions were higher for Black African, Black Caribbean and Black Other groups than for the rest of the population.

Rates of access to specialist mental health services are broadly higher for certain population groups. The Health & Social Care Information Centre states that people from the 'Black or Black British' ethnic group, which includes Caribbean, African and 'Any Other Black' ethnic categories, show the highest rates of access (13.7, 13.3 and 13.5 per 100 service users, respectively). As previously stated, around 70 per cent of inpatients in the Black or Black British ethnic groups were subject to a form of compulsory detention during 2012/13.

At-risk groups

Homeless Link estimates that around 70 per cent of people accessing homelessness services have a mental health problem. St Mungo's estimates that 64 per cent of its clients have drug and/or alcohol problems.

According to a study of 1,435 newly sentenced prisoners, 16 per cent of prisoners were reported to be experiencing symptoms indicative of psychosis. Nearly half were judged to be at risk of having anxiety or depression.

Physical health inequalities

People with a mental illness are almost twice as likely to die from coronary heart disease as the general population, four times more likely to die from respiratory disease, and are at a higher risk of being overweight or obese. Rethink Mental Illness estimates that a third of the 100,000 annual 'avoidable deaths' amongst the under-75s involve someone with a mental health problem.

Taking an inclusive definition of a mental health problem, which includes people with alcohol or illicit drug dependencies as well as conditions such as psychosis, about 42 per cent of all cigarettes smoked by the English population are smoked by people with a mental health problem.

Around 30 per cent of those suffering from a long-term physical health condition also have a mental health problem. The King's Fund estimates that between 12 and 18 per cent of NHS expenditure on the treatment and management of long-term conditions is linked to poor mental health and well-being.

Housing and employment

Compared with the general population, people with mental health conditions are one and a half times more likely to live in rented housing, with greater uncertainty about how long they can remain in their current home. People with mental health problems are twice as likely as those without a mental health condition to be unhappy with their housing and four times more likely to say that it makes their health worse. Mental ill health is frequently cited as a reason for tenancy breakdown and housing problems are often given as a reason for a person being admitted, or readmitted, to inpatient care.

Figures covering 2011/12 show that 8.9 per cent of adults in contact with secondary mental health services are in paid employment.

Workforce and staff satisfaction

There were 9,039 full-time equivalent (FTE) medical staff working within the psychiatry specialities in 2012, including 4,068 FTE consultants.

Respondents to the 2012 NHS staff survey from mental health and learning disability trusts reported the highest levels of job satisfaction, with an average of 3.66 out of five. This compared to an average of 3.62 out of five for staff working in commissioning organisations, 3.58 for respondents from acute trusts and 3.27 for people working in ambulance trusts. Respondents from mental health providers also expressed the largest level of satisfaction with support received from their immediate manager (71 per cent were 'satisfied' or 'very satisfied').

61 per cent of respondents to the NHS staff survey either agreed or strongly agreed that care of service users is their organisation's top priority. 81 per cent agreed or strongly agreed that their role makes a difference to service users. However, just 33 per cent either agreed or strongly agreed that sufficient staff were employed to enable them to do their work properly.

17 January 2014

⇨ The above information is reprinted with kind permission from The NHS Confederation. Please visit www.nhsconfed.org/MHN for further information. Visit the 'Resources' section of the website to download a copy of the Key Facts and trends in mental health – 2014 update with full references (http://www.nhsconfed.org/~/media/Confederation/Files/Publications/Documents/facts-trends-mental-health-2014.pdf).

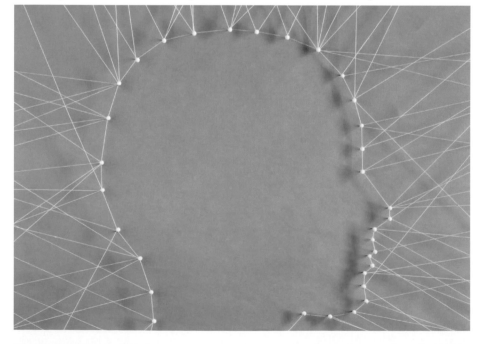

Misquoted and misunderstood: have 'one in four' people really had a mental health problem?

What do a government department, a charity, a Royal College and a journal paper all have in common?

By Joseph O'Leary

They've all quoted the same, widely used statistic: one in four people have experienced a mental health problem. And they've all sourced the figure to the same place: the 2007 Adult Psychiatric Morbidity Survey.

Except they don't all say the same thing:

⇨ Department of Health: 'At least one in four of us will experience a mental health problem at some point in our life.'

⇨ Mental Health Foundation: '1 in four people will experience some kind of mental health problem in the course of a year.'

⇨ Royal College of Psychiatrists: 'Almost one in four British adults… experience a diagnosable mental health problem at any given time.'

⇨ In the *British Medical Journal*: 'In 2007 the Annual Psychiatric Morbidity Survey (APMS) estimated a UK prevalence of 23% in the past week.'

We spoke to the authors of the 2007 study to find out why there might be such stark differences in interpretation.

The study itself is explicit about one of its main findings:

'in 2007 nearly one person in four (23 per cent) in England had at least one psychiatric disorder and 7.2 per cent had two or more disorders'.

In terms of this particular survey, that means about one in four adults met the criteria or screened positive for at least one of the psychiatric conditions or behaviours being studied. That includes, for instance: forms of anxiety, depression, phobias, eating disorders and drug or alcohol dependence.

The problem, as one of the authors informed us, is putting a time period on the figure. That's because not all the conditions being measured cover the same timeframe.

Anxiety and depression, for instance, were measured by identifying symptoms people demonstrated in the past week. Alcohol dependence refers to the past six months. Meanwhile drug dependence and eating disorders were measured based on the past year.

None, however, measured prevalence over a lifetime (the study did cover lifetime prevalence for some behaviours, but not for the purposes of this particular comparison).

So while the study pinpointed one in four having had a mental health problem, it confuses matters to assign a single time period to the claim, unless looking at a specific condition within.

An old relic

That said, the one in four claim also predates the 2007 Survey, so not all references to the figure necessarily refer to the recent findings. The earliest such reference we've found is, research paper dating back to 1980 by David Goldberg and Peter Huxley.

It gathered evidence suggesting that around 25% of people in 'community' samples (outside the care system at GP practices and hospitals) had some form of mental disorder in the past year. But importantly, this defined mental problems differently – excluding drug and alcohol dependence and more severe conditions such as schizophrenia.

Again, there was no measure of how many people had ever experienced a mental problem, and the authors themselves commented only a few years ago that looking at lifetime prevalence was:

'a highly questionable concept where common mental disorders are concerned, since it assumes that people not only can, but will reveal information about minor disorders that occurred many years ago, but that they have either forgotten or suppressed. For this reason, we have never quoted figures for life-time rates.

'However, for those that like to think in these terms, we would suggest that the figure of "at least 25%" is almost certainly a conservative figure.'

29 January 2014

⇨ The above information is reprinted with kind permission from Full Fact. Please visit www.fullfact.org for further information.

A good start in life

Most mental illness has its origins in childhood. The most important modifiable risk factors for mental illness and the most important determinants of mental well-being are childhood ones. The most important opportunities for prevention of mental illness and promotion of mental health therefore lie in childhood, many of them in the context of the family.

The figures on mental illness in childhood are stark:

⇨ half of all mental disorder first emerges before the age of 14 years and three quarters by age 25 years[1]

⇨ up to 25% of children show signs of mental health problems[2] more than half of which track through into adulthood

⇨ 10% of children have a clinically diagnosed mental disorder at any one point in childhood.[2] Only a minority of such children are in touch with services[2,3]

⇨ the most common childhood mental disorder is conduct disorder with a prevalence of 5%.[2]

Key risk factors are modifiable

The most important modifiable risk factor for mental health problems in childhood, and thus in adult life in general, is parenting. The key way to reduce risk in very early childhood is to promote healthy parenting focusing on the quality of parent-infant/child relationships, parenting styles including behaviour management, and infant and child nutrition (including breast-feeding and healthy eating). Parental mental illness and parental lifestyle behaviours such as smoking, and drug and alcohol misuse are important risk factors for childhood mental health problems.[4]

Schools offer another important opportunity for promotion and prevention. School, school ethos, bullying and teacher well-

There's a real family!

being all have an influence on children's current and future mental health. Mental health promotion programmes can modify these factors, and also mitigate mental health problems initiated from within the family.[5]

All the risk factors for mental illness also impact on cognitive development, leaving children doubly disadvantaged. Supporting children's emotional and social development is the most effective way to promote cognitive development and thus to mitigate the effect of educational inequality throughout the lifecourse.[6]

Science of parenting and brain development

The scientific underpinning of mental health promotion in childhood has been investigated in several different disciplines and is now quite well understood. Studies show how interactions between young children and their parents or primary care-givers profoundly influence the development of the many parts of the brain, particularly those involving emotional and social development, speech and language and the child's ability to manage life's stresses.

Poverty and deprivation

Poverty and deprivation make parenting more difficult, but high

quality parenting can protect against the effects of deprivation.[7] Abusive and neglectful parenting is associated statistically with poverty and deprivation,[8] but suboptimal parenting that is less damaging than abuse or neglect is distributed across the social spectrum.[9]

Parental mental illness and drug and alcohol misuse

The children most at risk of mental illness are those being raised in families where parents have a mental illness[10] or abuse drugs or alcohol. Standard parenting programmes may have limited impact where families are very dysfunctional. It is worthwhile improving parenting in such families and programmes are emerging which can do this.[11]

There are strong intergenerational links in mental illness, and genetic transmission is one of the non-modifiable risks. The expression of genetic risk is, however, influenced by the environment including parenting.[12,13]

Interventions

Childhood programmes represent by far the largest group of evidence-based approaches to promote mental health. A wide range of programmes has been developed and evaluated, and a very large evidence base has accumulated over the course of the last 60 years.

These cover universal, targeted and indicated approaches, and relate to interventions to support parenting and interventions to improve mental health in schools.

The majority of evidence-based parenting programmes address targeted or indicated populations. Some well-known parenting programmes combine parenting support with high-quality day care or school-based interventions. These programmes can improve both children's and parents' mental health and well-being. The extent of improvement which can be made in each generation is modest but worthwhile.

Targeting, though attractive, can be inefficient because there is no reliable way to identify high-risk groups; for example, parents with mental illness or parents who abuse drugs and alcohol. Current policy recommends universal underpinning and targeted provision for identifiable high-risk groups like teenage parents, or high-risk, socially disadvantaged areas.

Intervention research

Many different types of research are needed to tell whether interventions, programmes or approaches make a difference for whom, in what circumstances. Randomised controlled trials (RCT) are often difficult to carry out in health promoting settings and, whilst reducing some biases, may introduce others. Positive results are valuable, but may offer spuriously precise estimates of effect size, and negative results may not be able to distinguish between problems which ensue from trying to implement programmes in the context of an RCT and ineffective programmes.

Support for parenting and school mental health promotion features in much past and current public and child health policy. Provision varies throughout the UK and may be provided in health, education or third sector settings.

References

1) Kessler R, Berglund P, Demler O et al. Lifetime prevalence and age of onset distributions of DSM-VI disorders in the national comorbidity survey replication *Arch. Gen. Psych.* 2005 593–602

2) Green H, McGinnity A, Meltzer H, Ford T, Goodman, R. Mental health of children and young people in Great Britain, 2004 Palgrave Macmillan 2005

3) Sawyer MG, Arney FM, Baghurst PA et al. The mental health of young people in Australia: key findings from the child and adolescent component of the national survey of mental health and well-being. *Australian and New Zealand Journal of Psychiatry*; 35 806–814

4) Göpfert M, Webster J, Seema MV, (eds). Parental psychiatric disorder: distressed parents and their families. Cambridge, CUP 2004

5) Weare K. Promoting mental, emotional, and social health: a whole school approach. Psychology Press, 2000

6) National Research Council Institute of Medicine. From neurons to neighbourhoods: the science of early childhood. National Academy Press, 2000

7) Lempers JD, Calri-Lempers D, Simons R. Economic hardship, parenting and distress. *Child Development* 1989 60:25-39

8) Gingrich RD, Hudson JR. Child Abuse in a small city: social psychological and ecological correlates; *Journal of Sociology & Social Welfare* 376, 1981.

9) Waylen A, Stallard N, Stewart-Brown S. Parenting and social inequalities in health in mid-childhood: a longitudinal study. *European Journal of Public Health 2008* 18(3):300-305; doi:10.1093/eurpub/ckm131

10) Göpfert M, Webster J, Seema MV. Parental Psychiatric Disorder: distressed parents and their families. Cambridge University Press. 2004

11) Dawe S and Harnett P. Parenting under Pressure.

12) Dodge KA, Rutter M. Gene-environment Interactions in developmental psychopathology. Guilford Press. 2011

13) Kim-Cohen J, Caspi A, Taylor A, Williams B et al. MAOA, maltreatment, and gene–environment interaction predicting children's mental health: new evidence and a meta-analysis *Molecular Psychiatry* (2006); 11, 903–913

⇨ The above information is reprinted with kind permission from Faculty of Public Health. Please visit www.fph.org.uk for further information.

Mental health problems and well-being differences experienced by girls and boys

Well-being statements	Boys	Girls
I have felt suicidal	19%	33%
I have self-harmed	10%	28%
I have experienced panic attacks	12%	33%
I feel secure 'always' or 'often'	53%	48%
I have been prescribed anti-depressants	8%	14%
I feel happy with my mental health	59%	54%
I have experienced feelings of self-loathing	36%	54%
I have experienced insomnia	31%	43%
I feel inferior to others	31%	41%
I have had difficulty controlling my anger	17%	24%

Source: Girls at greater mental health risk, The Prince's Trust, 2014.

Does mental illness run in families?

Overview

This information may be useful if there is a history of mental illness in your family, and you are concerned that you may be also be affected. You may also find it useful if you have a mental illness yourself, and are concerned about the risk of your relatives having the same condition.

⇨ Some research does suggest that mental illness can run in families.

⇨ We do not fully understand what causes mental illness or why it can be passed on in family members.

⇨ Mental illness is probably passed on for a variety of factors, rather than just genes.

⇨ Although research might suggest that mental illness does run in families, it doesn't mean you or a family member are inevitably going to become unwell.

⇨ You might have questions if you are thinking of starting a family.

⇨ There are things we can all do to look after our mental health.

What is the risk of mental illness running in my family?

If someone in your family has a mental illness, you might be worried about developing the condition too. If you have a mental illness yourself, you might be worried that another relative will become unwell too.

Most people with a mental illness do not have relatives with the same illness. But research does suggest that it can run in families (see table below).

It also seems that different mental health conditions such as schizoaffective disorder and major depression can run in the same family. There is less evidence to show that other mental health conditions run in families.

What causes mental illness to run in families?

We do not fully understand what causes mental illness or why it can be passed on in family members. When a condition is passed on to other family members through genetics, it is known as being 'hereditary'.

Some research suggests that genetics directly cause some conditions like depression. As the table shows, the chances of developing a mental illness could depend on the closeness of the blood relationship with your relative. Although it does seem that mental illness can be hereditary, we do not fully understand how this works. Mental illness is probably passed on in family members for a variety of factors, rather than just genes.

Example

When an identical twin has a mental illness, the other twin does not always develop it too. If mental illness only had a genetic cause, then when one identical twin has a mental illness the other twin should always develop a mental illness as well. This is because identical twins share exactly the same genes.

Environmental factors such as isolation or a stressful life event can trigger the condition in someone who may already have a higher chance of developing a mental illness. However, even then it doesn't mean they are definitely going to develop an illness. Someone with no family history of mental illness can also develop a condition.

There are different ways of looking after your mental health which are explored further in the reducing risk section.

Starting a family

If you have a mental illness and are thinking of starting

What is the risk of mental illness running in my family?

The following table shows the chances of schizophrenia, bipolar disorder or psychosis being passed down through family members:

	Schizophrenia	Bipolar disorder	Psychosis
Lifetime chance (the chance of someone in the general population developing the condition during their lifetime)	1 in 100	Around 3 in 100	1 in 100
If one of your biological parents has the condition	13 in 100	15 in 100	10 in 100
If both of your biological parents have the condition	46 in 100	50 in 100	Information not included in source
If a sibling (brother or sister) or non-identical twin has the condition	10 in 100	13 in 100	10 in 100
If an identical twin has the condition	48 in 100	70 in 100	50 in 100
If a second degree relative has the condition (for example, aunt or uncle)	2 in 100	5 in 100	3 in 100

Source: What is the risk of mental illness running in my family?, Rethink, 2014.

a family, you could talk to a professional genetics counsellor. They can give specialist advice, support and information to families where relatives have certain health conditions. A GP or psychiatrist (if you have one) may be able to advise you of a service within your NHS Trust that provides genetic counselling. If you are thinking about adopting a child who has a family history of mental illness, you could also explore this option if you wanted more advice.

Is there anything I can do to reduce my risk of developing a mental illness?

Although research might suggest that mental illness does run in families, it doesn't mean you or a family member are inevitably going to become unwell. There are things we can all do to look after our mental health.

Things that you can do to look after your own mental health generally include:

Having a healthy diet

Eating a healthy balanced diet can make a difference to your mental and physical health. It can help make you less likely to become unwell as well as help you stay at a healthy body weight.

Taking regular exercise

Moderate exercise can help to improve your mood and how you feel generally. It can also help you to feel better about yourself.

Getting enough sleep

Problems with sleep can affect how you feel physically and mentally. In turn, how you feel can also affect how you sleep. If you regularly have problems sleeping, then you could discuss this with your GP.

Talking to someone about your problems

Talking to people about any problems you have can be useful. There are a number of ways that you can offload or chat to someone about how you're feeling. Many services offer telephone, email or instant messaging chat. Some of these are listed in the useful contacts section on the rethink website.

Learning more about something that interests you

Think about things that you enjoy doing. This could be a hobby, attending classes or volunteering.

Stress

Try to avoid too much stress as far as possible. A lot of things in life can cause stress which can impact on mental health.

'Environmental factors such as isolation or a stressful life event can trigger [a] condition in someone who may already have a higher chance of developing a mental illness'

Drug use

Using alcohol or drugs can trigger mental illness in some people. It can also cause further problems with getting the right treatment if you do become unwell. If you find you use alcohol or drugs to deal with your problems or stress, then you could explore some of the other options above instead.

If you are concerned that you are experiencing signs of mental illness, you could speak to your GP about this.

August 2013

⇨ The above information is reprinted with kind permission from Rethink Mental Illness. Please visit www.rethink.org for further information.

Caring for someone with a mental illness

As many as one in four people experience some form of mental health problem. Caring for someone with mental health problems brings unique challenges.

Mental health problems vary greatly in severity. Mild problems are common and can be helped with understanding and support. Severe mental illness, such as deep depression, is less common and poses more challenges.

Communicating with someone with a mental illness

Communication can be a struggle for many people with a mental illness. Some people don't have the motivation to communicate, while others lack the confidence to say what they really want. Some people experience hallucinations, which can affect how and when they communicate.

To help the person you care for communicate, give them enough time to make themselves heard and let them know that you accept them and their illness.

Often, people with mental health problems feel cut off from other people, including family, friends and neighbours. It's important to listen to what they've got to say and let them express themselves without interrupting or offering your opinion. Encourage and reassure them if they get upset or appear to be struggling with their emotions.

You may have known the person you care for before they had their mental illness. It's important to remember that they just happen to be going through a period of mental distress.

Getting a diagnosis of mental illness

If you care for someone who appears to have a mental health problem, they may not have sought medical advice or they may be struggling to get a specific diagnosis. Do not diagnose mental health problems yourself. A mental health diagnosis will usually be made by a psychiatrist with input from other healthcare professionals.

Getting a definite diagnosis of a mental illness can be difficult as there are no definitive physical tests. A diagnosis will usually be made by collecting lists of symptoms and a medical history. As a carer, you may also be asked to describe your experience of their illness.

If the person you care for doesn't agree with their initial diagnosis, they can get a second opinion.

Confidentiality and mental illness

People who care for someone with a mental illness may find that some healthcare professionals are reluctant or unwilling to share information with them. This can be very frustrating as very often the carer has the fullest picture of the person's condition. Mental healthcare professionals are legally bound to protect the confidentiality of their patients, so they may be unable, rather than unwilling, to talk about care needs.

To deal with this problem, try to get the consent of the person you care for to discuss their care needs as early as possible after their diagnosis. This consent should be made clear on any care plans or documentation relating to their care, and any changes to this consent should be clearly noted.

Mental healthcare professionals may not be able tell you certain personal details about the mental health of the person you care for, but this doesn't mean that they should not listen to your perspective.

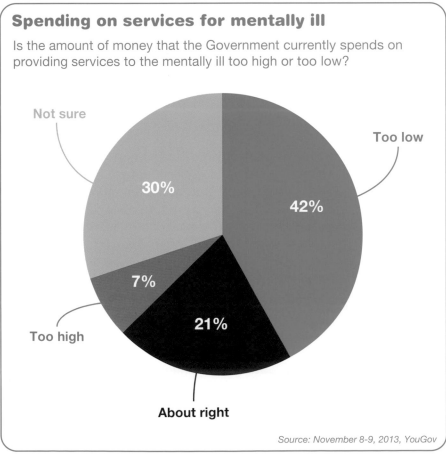

Spending on services for mentally ill

Is the amount of money that the Government currently spends on providing services to the mentally ill too high or too low?

Not sure — 30%

Too low — 42%

Too high — 7%

About right — 21%

Source: November 8-9, 2013, YouGov

Dealing with behaviour caused by mental illness

If the person you care for is feeling particularly isolated or desperate, they may say that they want to kill themselves or they may attempt to do it.

Mentioning suicide may not be the same thing as a person wanting to end their life. They may say that they feel overwhelmed and want it to end, or talk about feeling useless or that their life is pointless. It's important to acknowledge such statements rather than being dismissive or making light of them.

You may be worried about your safety, or the safety of the person you care for or someone else. In this case, consider getting an assessment under the Care Programme Approach for the person you care for, as well as a carer's assessment for yourself.

If you believe that you or anyone else is in immediate danger, contact social services to get an assessment. If you can't contact anyone in the crisis team at your local social services, call 999 and ask for an ambulance to take them to the accident and emergency (A&E) department of a local hospital.

The person you care for should be consulted at every stage of treatment and can only have treatment or tests with their consent, unless they're detained under the Mental Health Act.

Support and resources for carers of people with mental illness

If you're struggling to care for someone with a mental health problem, it may help to talk to other carers in a similar situation. Some local carers' organisations have separate meetings for carers of people with mental health problems.

For details of your nearest carers' support group, call Carers Direct on 0300 123 1053. Lines are open 9am to 8pm Monday to Friday and 11am to 4pm weekends (closed on bank holidays).

The mental health charity Rethink offers a number of specialist services across the country for carers of people with severe mental illness. It also has more than 138 groups that meet regularly to give carers and people with severe mental illness a support network in their local area.

The person you care for may become increasingly reliant on you. It's common for people with a mental health diagnosis, such as depression, to become insular and lose interest in social activities. You may be one of the few people they have contact with.

It's important to maintain your social activities. You may need to have a conversation with the person you care for about what you're prepared to do and what you're not prepared to do. You may need to be firm with your decision. If you feel you're doing too much, see if someone else can share the caring responsibility with you.

Looking after yourself as a carer of someone with a mental illness

Although it's important to support the person you care for, it's essential to look after your own mental health too. If you start to feel depressed or anxious and getting support hasn't helped, it may be time to speak to your GP about the impact your caring role is having on your mental health.

Call Carers Direct on 0300 123 1053

Confidential information and advice for carers.

Lines are open 9am to 8pm Monday to Friday (except bank holidays), 11am to 4pm at weekends. Request a free call back or an interpreted call back in one of more than 170 languages.

You can talk to an adviser live online or send a query by email.

⇨ The above information is reprinted with kind permission from NHS Choices. Please visit www.nhs.uk for further information.

© NHS Choices 2014

Mental health cuts costing NHS millions

A report highlighted the rising pressures on the mental health trusts to provide care for patients with a diminishing budget. The mental health trust budget rose to its highest in 2011/12 but referrals also rose by 13%. Last year's budget fell by 2.3%, despite higher demand.

This correlates to the community mental health teams, who provide long-term support to patients, being asked to save almost 20% more for next year's budget than hospitals.

Rethink Mental Illness published the report with the London School of Economics. In this tough economic situation, the value of service is increasingly important. Minister of State for Care and Support, Norman Lamb, called for a 'shift of resources' to preventive care and said that the Government had given NHS England a 'clear objective' to put mental and physical health on a par.

The report suggested that a reallocation of the budget could help alleviate the situation. For example, 54% of the psychosis budget was being spent on inpatient care rather than preventative services.

The report said mental health accounted for 23% of the disease burden in England but only received 12% of the health budget

Early intervention could save money in later stages

It costs £13 a day to support someone with psychosis or schizophrenia in the community. If they were to stay in hospital it would cost £350 a day. Another example of the difference in cost, is the £1,000 the NHS saves every time someone is treated with cognitive behavioural therapy instead of being in hospital.

Norman Lamb, said that early access to treatment in the community was 'often the best option' for people with psychosis and schizophrenia.

He also said patients 'benefit from being in familiar surroundings among loved ones' and are 'less likely to need costly hospital stays'.

Dr Martin McShane, national director for long-term conditions at NHS England, said the report was 'very helpful' and was supportive of what the organisation wanted to achieve.

10 April 2014

⇨ The above information is reprinted with kind permission from Healthcare Today. Please visit www.healthcare-today.co.uk for further information.

mental health care
DEMAND

mental health care
FUNDING

'The beds crisis makes me embarrassed to work in mental health': a social worker's story

An extract from a letter sent to Community Care by a frontline social worker and approved mental health professional.

By an anonymous social worker

We always have high bed occupancy on our acute admissions units to the extent that we have over 40 people in out-of-area beds, some as far away as 175 miles from home. We recently had a psychiatric unit closed and now our trust is spending millions on out-of-area beds.

The impact this has on patients and families is devastating. Service users and families often find journeys of a few miles to one of our remaining NHS units difficult. Imagine what it's like when we ask them to travel to out-of-area beds close to 200 miles away?

One family member reported having a 15-hour round trip to go and visit someone. This means that people are not being visited by families and friends when they need it.

In my experience, right now people have absolutely no chance of an informal admission to hospital (as opposed to a compulsory admission under the Mental Health Act) because there are no beds for them.

'People are being discharged prematurely because of the constant pressure on beds'

So people who could have been admitted voluntarily at an early stage in their crisis are instead left in the community while their mental health deteriorates to the point they may need to be admitted under the Mental Health Act for a long admission.

The beds situation impacts us as approved mental health professionals (AMHPs) and community social workers but is also impacts NHS ward staff too.

They have no say in decisions to move patients from ward to ward. Instead these calls are made by managers with nothing to do with the day-to-day running of the ward but focused on crunching numbers.

Shifting people about like this harms continuity of care for patients and it harms any therapeutic work or relationship that staff have built up with patients. It must feel soul destroying.

I've noticed wards also seem more chaotic when they are over-occupied. Ward rounds, ward business and hospital targets are pushed up the agenda at the expense of one-to-one time with patients.

It damages staff morale. Frontline workers are too stressed to function how they would like to. So sickness rates are high and wards turn to agency staff to fill gaps (again impacting the continuity and consistency of care).

'One family member reported having a 15-hour round trip to go and visit someone'

From my point of view as an AMHP and social worker, I have turned up to ward rounds to be told that the patient I was here for has been moved to another ward on another hospital because they had to use a bed for another patient.

In the increasingly rare situation where a bed for someone who needs to be admitted to hospital can be found in our area, we are frequently told that the bed is 'an unsafe leave bed'. This means that when we fill the bed a detained person on leave would not be able to return to the ward if they needed to.

People are also being discharged prematurely because of the constant pressure on beds. This has led to re-admissions after only a few days in some cases because inpatient teams – under pressure to free-up beds – have not listened to community staff when they have warned that the person is not ready for discharge.

It's stuff like this that makes me embarrassed to work in mental health and it's a shame because I feel like a lot of what I have written about here is outside of my control. I also think that there are a lot of very caring and experienced people working my area. It is horrible that any of us should need to feel ashamed by the circumstances in which we practise.

16 October 2013

⇨ The above information is reprinted with kind permission from Community Care. Please visit www.communitycare.co.uk for further information.

Number of UK war veterans seeking help for mental health issues on the rise

Combat Stress charity reports 57% increase in number of ex-military personnel needing treatment in 2013 and says UK must prepare for escalation.

By Nick Hopkins

The number of Afghanistan veterans seeking help for mental health problems surged in 2013 and is likely to peak again this year as the British military ends its 13-year conflict in the country, according to new figures published on Monday.

There was a 57% increase in the number of ex-military personnel needing treatment from the charity Combat Stress, which had a record 358 Afghanistan-related referrals last year, compared with 228 in 2012.

The number of Iraq veterans needing help also rose by nearly 20%, even though British troops ended combat operations in the country five years ago, and left altogether in 2011.

Commodore Andrew Cameron, chief executive of Combat Stress, added that he expected the numbers to further increase over the coming years and the UK had to prepare for the escalation. Most mental health issues take time to emerge, and armed forces veterans are often unwilling to admit they need help.

'These statistics show that, although the Iraq war ended in 2011 and troops are withdrawing from Afghanistan later this year, a significant number of veterans who serve in the armed forces continue to relive the horrors they experienced on the frontline or during their time in the armed forces,' Cameron said. 'Day in, day out, they battle these hidden psychological wounds, often tearing families apart in the process.'

Even now, Combat Stress is taking on new cases from veterans who fought in conflicts from an earlier generation, such as the Malayan Emergency, which ended in 1960, and the 1982 Falklands war.

But the vast majority of its current caseload of 5,400 patients comprises veterans from Iraq, Afghanistan and Northern Ireland, with sharp rises in referrals from all three in recent years.

Cameron said that one-fifth of all veterans were likely to need help for some form of mental illness and that it could take more than a decade before symptoms presented themselves. 'They have faced unique challenges and require, and deserve, specialist support to help them overcome these challenges. However, with demand for our services already rising, Combat Stress faces a real challenge. We are planning for services at or above the current level for at least the next five years, and we do not expect to see demand for support tail off in the near future,' he said.

Combat Stress compiled the statistics to mark its 95th anniversary. It has worked with veterans of every conflict since the Second World War, and has found that, on average, servicemen and women wait 13 years after leaving the military before seeking help. It has supported 20,326 veterans, including soldiers, sailors and air crews who fought in Aden, Korea and the Iran-Iraq war. More than 83% of those needing treatment have served in the army, and 3% of the total are women.

Military charities are bracing themselves for an increase in referrals now that the Afghanistan conflict is drawing to a close, with conditions ranging from depression to post-traumatic stress disorder.

Combat Stress said it had only one referral in the first year of the conflict in 2003 and two the year after. But with tens of thousands of troops having deployed to the country over the past decade, those numbers have increased sharply, particularly over the past three years.

It estimates that 42,000 UK troops who served in Iraq and Afghanistan may develop a mental health condition over the coming decades.

The charity has treated 1,300 Afghanistan veterans so far and has 662 in its care. It has received 1,968 cases involving Iraq veterans and is treating 806.

General Sir Richard Dannatt, chief of the general staff when British forces were fighting in Iraq and Afghanistan, said: 'There is no doubt that combat, whether in Northern Ireland, the Falklands, the Gulf war 90–91, Bosnia, and elsewhere, has always produced psychiatric casualties, just as it produced 'shell shock' in the First World War.

'Our operations in Iraq and Afghanistan have, and will, produce a sharp upturn in such psychiatric casualties. How many, no one really knows.

'The Ministry of Defence will always try to talk the figure down for budgetary and compensation reasons. But psychiatric injuries should be widely recognised and talked about.'

Dannatt said that former soldiers were often caught up in a 'culture of coping alone' and that it needed to be recognised that there were too many former combatants who ended up in jail as murderers, or as suicide victims.

He argued that it was necessary to make mental health treatment more rapidly available: 'If you break a leg, you don't wait six weeks for a fracture clinic appointment. The same must apply in the mental health area.'

The MoD has launched several campaigns to challenge the stigma associated with mental health problems, including one called 'Don't Bottle it Up'. It has provided funding for Combat Stress – and more community psychiatric nurses are being hired to boost community outreach teams.

'We are committed to giving everyone who serves in our armed forces all the help and support they need,' a government spokesman said, adding that £7.4 million had been invested to improve mental health services available to former soldiers. It was the aim of the Government 'to further reduce the stigma of mental illness' and to encourage more veterans in need to come forward.

The Tory donor and peer Lord Ashcroft was commissioned by the Prime Minister, David Cameron, to write a review of services for armed forces veterans, which was published in February.

He said that greater awareness of the problems faced by veterans 'may be contributing to the perception of a bow wave of PTSD cases'.

He added: 'There is a widespread public perception that veterans are likely to be physically, mentally or emotionally damaged by their time in the armed forces. This in itself constitutes an unnecessary extra hurdle for service leavers, restricting their opportunities by lowering expectations of what they can do.'

12 May 2014

⇨ The above information is reprinted with kind permission from *The Guardian*. Please visit www.theguardian.com for further information.

Mental health and well-being in the workplace

Ignoring mental health in the workplace doesn't make good business sense – research shows that FTSE 100 companies that prioritise employee engagement and well-being outperform the rest of the FTSE 100 by 10%.

We know that performance and effectiveness at work is largely dependent on mental health and well-being – with as many as one in four of us experiencing problems with our mental health in the course of a year, organisations understand that this is an important issue for them and their staff.

Mental health and well-being in the workplace

Mental health and well-being has moved up the agenda for employers. Growing research demonstrates the importance of mental health and well-being in relation to our performance and effectiveness at work. There are clear links between our physical and mental health that further supports the case for protecting mental health and well-being at work too. Poor mental health is associated with an increased risk of diseases such as cardiovascular disease, cancer and diabetes, while good mental health is a known protective factor. Poor physical health also increases the risk of people developing mental health problems.

Employers should expect that at any one time nearly one in six of their workforce is affected by a mental health problem. A study carried out by the University of Strathclyde on behalf of the Scottish Trades Union Congress (STUC) reported that on average employees take 21 days for each period of absence related to mental health. Mental health problems cost Scottish employers over £2 billion a year.

Stress, depression and anxiety are reported as the most common reasons for staff absence – however, a lot of the mental health absence that is work related could

Employment and mental health

40% **62%**

...of British employers would hire someone with...

...a mental health condition

...a physical condition

Source: Mental health – The Facts, New Internationalist magazine, May 2012

1 in 6 workers will experience a mental health problem

Source: Time to Change, 2014

70 million working days were lost to mental illness last year

The number of working days lost to **stress, depression** and **anxiety** has **risen by 24%** since 2009

Source: More has to be done to help people with mental health problems stay in work, The Guardian, 9 September 2014.

have been prevented. Evidence shows that there are a number of simple, cost-effective ways to support employee mental health.

Employers could consider measures to support and protect employee well-being:

⇨ Flexible working options

⇨ Effectively 'mental health'-trained managers

⇨ Raising awareness and creating an open culture to discuss mental health

⇨ Involving employees in decision making

⇨ Integrating mental health and well-being throughout policies and procedures

⇨ Introducing stress risk management procedures

⇨ Providing access to employee assistance programmes and occupational health

⇨ Having regular meetings with managers

⇨ Introducing performance management processes

⇨ Conducting return to work interviews.

Employers' responsibilities around stress

Stress, although not a diagnosable medical condition, is a major contributor to a range of physical and mental health problems. The sources of stress, if not addressed, can lead to long term, debilitating health problems and lengthy absences from the workplace.

Employers have a responsibility to support staff who may be experiencing stress, either work-related, or otherwise. They also have a duty to ensure that risks arising from work activity are properly controlled. The Health and Safety Executive's *Management Standards for Tackling Work-Related Stress*, highlight the following aspects of work which may affect staff stress levels:

⇨ demands

⇨ control

⇨ support

⇨ relationships

⇨ roles

⇨ change.

By managing these organisational aspects of work, and reducing levels of stress in the workforce,

employers will see the benefits in the form of:

⇨ increased productivity

⇨ reduction in accident levels

⇨ lower sickness absence rates

⇨ lower staff turnover

⇨ improved staff morale.

Tackling the stigma and discrimination of mental health problems

Tackling the stigma and discrimination of mental health problems in the workplace means that employers can make a positive impact on the lives of people who are experiencing, or have experienced, mental health problems.

Challenging negative assumptions about mental health problems and the ability to recover from them helps everyone, and can mean that staff are more likely to seek help earlier and recover more quickly.

Scotland's anti-stigma campaign, 'See Me', has a range of free resources, including posters and leaflets, that can be displayed in the workplace to stimulate discussion and help improve attitudes.

Workplace training – 'Mentally Healthy Workplace' training

Line managers are key to supporting and promoting the mental health and well-being of employees. Over a number of years, Healthy Working Lives – in partnership with employers, mental health service users and expert advisers – has developed a training package specifically for line managers. The course teaches us how to develop mentally healthy workplaces, including tackling stigma and discrimination, managing personal stress, supportive management practices and the legal requirements under the Equality Act (2010).

23 June 2014

⇨ The above information is reprinted with kind permission from Healthy Working Lives. Please visit www.healthyworkinglives. com for further information.

© NHS Health Scotland 2014

My experience of talking about mental health in a Muslim community

By Habiba

I have always struggled to talk to my family about my mental health problems openly because I was scared I would not get the support that I need but obviously when you live in the same house, you cannot hide it from them. I live with an eating disorder, social anxiety disorder and depression, which my family find hard to take in. This has left me feeling like I am fighting this by myself and unfortunately, because I have very little support from loved ones, I am not getting any better.

In my experience, mental illness is a very taboo subject in Islam

You could argue that it is a taboo subject in general but, specifically in Islam, I have found that it can be incredibly difficult for family members to understand.

'The stigma has left me feeling rather lost and alone and like I have no one to turn to. Family is an important part in recovery and when you feel like you cannot talk to the people who you live with, your world seems even darker than it already is'

For me, this has always been the case. I did not open up to family members about this issue for a long time because I was ashamed to even admit it to them. I was afraid of their reaction and thought they would neglect me. So, after speaking to my eating disorder treatment team about being afraid to speak to my family, they offered to sit down with my family and explain to them about why I have this condition and what they are doing to help me, which has helped my family understand a little bit and reassured them that I can get better. I was surprised by their reaction. It was not as bad as I thought it would be. Now, it is easier for me to talk to my family about it but they still find it hard to understand fully.

Support is what I need

An eating disorder affects the whole family, not just the sufferer. If I could control it, I would stop this right now and decide to get better to put my family at rest but it is not as simple as that. To my family, I am the one who is 'crazy' because I have mental health issues. I know they care and they do not understand the reasons behind why things are so hard for me. If they did, they would not think like they do. Support is what I need. They do not like to admit that I am suffering. It is very much like I am a different person to them, whom they wish was not abnormal. I seem to have become such a burden to my family and that makes me feel incredibly guilty.

This stigma has left me feeling rather lost and alone and like I have no one to turn to. Family is an important part in recovery and when you feel like you cannot talk to the people who you live with, your world seems even darker than it already is.

There is nothing wrong in asking for help

I think some Muslim families neglect the issue of mental illness because of a feeling that it brings shame on them and the reputation of the family. In Islam, we rely on God to heal us. If we are depressed or ill, we pray to God to make us better. We do our five prayers every day and make du'aa (invocation) whenever possible. If you are a spiritual and faithful person and rely on God to make you better, then there is nothing wrong with that at all. I think that believing in a higher power when feeling down is the most amazing thing to have in you. However, combining proper treatment to get to the root of the illness will make the sufferer see things in a new light. God will always be there to turn to but, sometimes, we need to talk openly about our problems to someone who can help us practically as well as emotionally and create a support network of friends and family.

There is nothing wrong in asking for help. There is nothing wrong in going to your GP and admitting that you are experiencing a mental health problem and that you need psychological help.

'Specifically in Islam, I have found that it can be incredibly difficult for family members to understand [mental illness]'

I live within a big Muslim community and there is hardly any talk about mental illness. It is as if the problem does not exist. In fact, it seems like it should not exist because people are so ashamed of it and that makes me feel ashamed to even have an illness. We need to start talking.

22 October 2013

⇨ The above information is reprinted with kind permission from Time To Change. Please visit www.time-to-change.org.uk for further information on this and other subjects.

Children treated on adult mental health wards on the rise

More children and young people have been treated on adult mental health wards in the first eight months of 2013/14 than the whole of the previous year, new data reveals.

By Derren Hayes

Provisional data published yesterday by the Health and Social Care Information Centre (HSCIC) shows that between April and November 2013, 250 under-18s were recorded as spending time on adult mental health wards as a result of 303 admissions to hospital.

Over the eight-month period, child admissions accounted for 10,424 bed days on adult wards. North Essex Partnership NHS Foundation Trust and Tees, Esk and Wear Valleys NHS Foundation Trust had the highest number of young people treated on adult wards, while Southern Health NHS Foundation Trust had the most bed days.

Under the Mental Health Act (2007) adult mental health wards are deemed to be inappropriate settings for treating under-18s, and a succession of government ministers have pledged over recent years to end their use for children and young people.

Campaigners have seized on the figures as further evidence of a 'crisis' in children's mental health services. Lucie Russell, director of campaigns at YoungMinds said: 'It is totally unacceptable that the numbers of children being treated on adult wards is on the increase. The legislation clearly states that an adult mental health ward is not an appropriate setting for vulnerable children with mental health problems.

'Unfortunately this issue reflects a crisis in mental health services across the board – from early intervention services to inpatient care. Young people are suffering increasing distress and yet services are being cut.

'Urgent action must be taken to ensure that the worrying increase in children on adult wards is halted and that both early intervention and crisis services improve.'

In 2012/13, there were 219 under-18s treated on adult mental health wards, a drop of 39 per cent on the previous year. The number of bed days also fell 46 per cent to 11,791 in 2012/13, while admissions were also significantly lower.

Under the 2007 Act, young people aged 16 and 17 are only meant to be treated in adult wards in exceptional circumstances, such as when waiting for a bed on a child ward to become available, while children under 16 should never be admitted to them. However, the HSCIC

data shows that in the first eight months of 2013/14 there were 31 under-16s treated on adult wards, up from 23 in the whole of 2012/13.

Norman Lamb, Care and Support Minister, said: 'Children and young people should not be treated on adult mental health wards. Our mental health crisis care concordat makes clear that the NHS must treat people under 18 in an environment suitable for their age, according to their needs.

'We've also invested £54 million to transform services, giving children and young people improved access to the best mental health care.'

Dr Jacqueline Cornish, NHS England's national clinical director for children, young people and transition to adulthood, said: 'Children and young people with mental health problems being treated in adult settings is totally unacceptable in the majority of cases.

'We recognise there is an issue around bed availability within Tier 4 child and adolescent mental health services, where we see the most seriously ill patients, which we are working hard to address.'

12 March 2014

⇨ The above information is reprinted with kind permission from Children & Young People Now. Please visit www.cypnow.co.uk for further information.

Number of under-18s treated on adult wards:

April-November 2013:	250
2012/13:	219
2011/12:	357

Number of bed days of under-18s treated on adult wards:

April-November 2013:	10,424
2012/13:	11,791
2011/12:	21,980

Source: Children treated on adult mental health wards on the rise, Children & Young People Now 2014.

Rise in use of the Mental Health Act, regulator finds

CQC publishes its fourth Mental Health Act Report

The number of people detained or treated under the Mental Health Act (MHA) has risen by 12 per cent in the last five years, the Care Quality Commission (CQC) says in its fourth *Mental Health Act Annual Report*, published today.

The Act was used 50,000 times to detain or treat people under compulsion last year, the report says, and there were 45,000 uses of the Act in 2008/9.

Examples of outstanding care were also found over the year, with inspectors seeing people with mental health problems benefiting from high-quality and safe psychiatric care that respects their dignity.

However, access to crisis care remains inadequate and health-based places of safety* for people experiencing a mental health crisis are often not staffed at all times, the report finds.

Some health-based places of safety have been found to be empty while patients are taken to police custody, and this contradicts the fundamental principles of the Act that urge the least restrictive care.

CQC chief executive David Behan said: 'We have seen great advances in treatment and care for people with mental health needs in recent years. We have also met staff committed to reducing the restrictions placed on patients as far as possible.

'However, we are concerned that access to crisis care is still a problem and that police custody is used when people should be in health-based places of safety. This needs to improve.

'We're also asking hospitals, other providers and commissioners to act on these findings and make sure that people receive high-quality, safe care.'

People with mental health problems in a crisis should have an emergency service that equals in speed and quality to that provided to people with a physical health emergency.

The MHA report does not include findings from inspections carried out under the Health and Social Care Act, although these two inspection programmes are merging.

CQC chief inspector of hospitals Mike Richards said: 'We're committed to making sure people detained or treated under the Act get the least restrictive care possible and that this care is the highest possible quality and designed around the individual needs of the patient.

'These people have the right to safe and respectful care. This is why we are changing the way we inspect, to make sure patients have positive experiences as far as possible during what can be very challenging and distressing periods in their lives.'

Other findings in the MHA report include:

⇨ One or more blanket rule was in place in more than three quarters of the wards we visited – this is unacceptable. These rules most commonly apply to Internet or mobile phone use, smoking, access to outdoor space or communal rooms, withholding post or phone calls

⇨ Some patients' physical health needs were not met; of 550 records examined, we found 14 per cent were on a ward with no access to a GP service

⇨ Staffing levels were linked to the quality of care in some places, with inadequate staffing preventing patients from taking leave and also exacerbating problem behaviour

⇨ Examples of patients in seclusion with inadequate regard for their privacy and dignity

⇨ More than a quarter of care plans showed no evidence of patients being involved in creating them

⇨ Around a third of care plans do not show evidence of discharge planning – this means detention periods could be inappropriately long.

CQC inspections on the use of the MHA use teams of specialists as well as 'experts by experience', who are people who have experience of using mental health services.

Notes

⇨ *Health-based places of safety are assessment suites in mental health hospitals and acute accident and emergency departments.

⇨ CQC is carrying out a dedicated review to find out more about how crisis mental health care is provided in an emergency. This will publish this year.

About the Care Quality Commission

The Care Quality Commission (CQC) is the independent regulator of health and social care in England.

We make sure health and social care services provide people with safe, effective, compassionate, high-quality care and we encourage care services to improve.

We monitor, inspect and regulate services to make sure they meet fundamental standards of quality and safety and we publish what we find to help people choose care.

20 May 2014

⇨ The above information is reprinted with kind permission from Care Quality Commission. Please visit www.cqc.org.uk for further information.

Nick Clegg announces NHS to put mental health issues on same footing as cancer

Nick Clegg has announced suicidal patients will be given the same priority as heart attack victims as part of an effort to increase resources for those with mental health problems.

Waiting times for mentally ill patients in England will be introduced for the first time with some conditions being put on the same footing as cancer.

Most people with depression who need talking therapies will begin treatment within six weeks.

Young people hit by psychosis for the first time should be seen within two weeks – the same target as cancer patients – when the changes come into force next April.

Clegg will tell activists at the Liberal Democrat party conference in Glasgow the £120 million plan is the first step in reforming 'Cinderella' mental health services.

Liberal Democrats would extend reforms to other areas, such as bipolar and eating disorders, in a future government using half of the extra £1 billion that would be raised from tax measures hitting the wealthiest that they would plough into the NHS.

The Deputy Prime Minister will use his keynote speech today to put the shake-up at the heart of the Lib Dem general election campaign – even though he concedes the move will not be popular with all of his party.

Clegg will tell activists: 'For the first time ever, we will introduce national waiting times for patients with mental health conditions.

'Labour introduced waiting times in physical health – we will do the same

for the many people struggling with conditions that you often can't see, that we often don't talk about, but which are just as serious.

'So if you are waiting for talking therapies to help with your depression, you will be seen within six weeks – 18 weeks at an absolute maximum – just as if you are waiting for an operation on your hip.

'If you are a young person experiencing psychosis for the first time, you will be seen within two weeks, something we are going to roll out across the country – just as if you suspect you have cancer.

'If you are having a breakdown, if you are thinking of harming yourself, for any emergency which takes you to A&E, you'll get the help you need – just as if you had gone to hospital with chest pains or following an accident.

'These are big, big changes. And in government again the Liberal Democrats will commit to completing this overhaul of our mental health services, ending the discrimination against mental health for good.

'And while I know not everyone in the party is going to agree, I can tell you now, I want this smack bang on the front page of our next manifesto.'

Aides said Clegg has not suffered from any mental illness but has campaigned on improving treatment for patients his 'whole political career' after seeing first hand as an MP the struggle some people have.

Mental health problems are estimated to cost the economy around £100 billion a year and around 70 million working days are also lost annually.

Clegg will say: 'I have campaigned to end the Cinderella treatment of mental health services ever since, because it threatens the opportunities available to hundreds and thousands of our fellow citizens.

'Anxiety, panic attacks, depression, anorexia, bulimia, self-harm, bipolar disorder – these and many other mental health conditions are one of the last remaining taboos in our society, and yet they will affect one in four people.

'Much progress has been made – people now speak out in the way they never did before, we have put mental health on the same legal footing in the NHS as physical health, we're massively expanding talking therapies and transforming the help children can get as they move into adulthood – but there's still a long, long way to go.

'I want this to be a country where a young dad chatting at the school gates will feel as comfortable discussing anxiety, stress, depression as the mum who's explaining how she sprained her ankle.'

Mark Winstanley, chief executive officer at Rethink Mental Illness, said: 'This is a watershed moment for everyone affected by mental illness and has the potential to improve the lives of millions.

'No one should have to wait months or even years for potentially life-changing treatment, just because they have a mental health problem rather than a physical one. Together with our supporters, we have been campaigning for maximum waiting times for many years.'

Sarah Brennan, chief executive of YoungMinds, said: 'We welcome this announcement, which is really good news in terms of confronting the glaring gaps in the parity of esteem between physical and mental health services especially around waiting times.

'We also warmly welcome the financial resources being put into inpatient care and the five-year plan for improving mental health services.'

Centre for Mental Health chief executive Sean Duggan said: 'The provision of additional funding to invest in crisis care and early intervention should help to overcome the current postcode lottery in access to these essential health services.'

NHS England estimated the cost to the UK of mental illness to be as much as £100 billion each year through lost working days, benefits and treating preventable illness as a result of mental illness and expected the plan to claw back some savings.

These include £44 million per year saved due to reduced hospital admissions for psychosis patients, around £5 million saved through improved A&E psychiatric liaison services and a reduction in the estimated 70 million working days lost.

Simon Stevens, NHS England's chief executive, said: 'This is an important moment when we will bring parity of esteem for mental health services a step closer. Putting access and waiting standards in place across all mental health services, and delivering better integration of physical and mental health care by 2020, will bring us much closer towards that aim.'

Dr Geraldine Strathdee, NHS England's national clinical director for mental health, said: 'This programme will start the journey to transform mental health care in England. Today people who present in crisis often wait too long for an assessment and to access treatment.

'This new approach will help improve crisis care and help reduce the distress that untreated mental illness brings. With 75% of long-term mental health problems diagnosed before 18, investing in early effective treatments will pay immediate and long-term dividends.'

Health Minister Norman Lamb said it was 'outrageous' that mental health patients did not have the same waiting time targets as people with other conditions.

He told BBC Radio 4's *Today* programme: 'This is a simple fact of discrimination. If you have cancer you

get access to a specialist within two weeks. If you have a first episode of psychosis it's completely haphazard.

'That is outrageous. There's both a moral and an economic case to do this.'

He said the Lib Dems will press for extra funding for the NHS in Chancellor George Osborne's Autumn Statement. 'We have been very clear that the NHS needs more funding. We are the only party that's come out and said that in 2015/16, in other words next year, the NHS needs a funding boost.

'It will be our top priority for the Autumn Statement to argue the case for extra funding.'

Lamb, who has been tipped as a potential successor to Clegg, insisted that 'nobody' had said the Deputy Prime Minister was not up to the job.

But he said he would consider a run for the leadership once Clegg decides to stand down.

He said: 'I am a very, very strong supporter of Nick. I think, in time, people will recognise the extraordinarily important role he has played, and in delivering political stability at a time of economic distress, that is a priceless commodity.

'I absolutely don't want to replace Nick Clegg.

'When he stands down, I haven't ruled out standing for the leadership myself. That's the extent of it. We'll cross that bridge when we come to it, in the meantime I think he has performed brilliantly in government, securing this country's economic future.'

8 October 2014

⇨ The above information is reprinted with kind permission from Press Association. Please visit www.pressassociation.com for further information.

Mental health pledge welcomed, but when will it help teens?

A government pledge to improve access to mental health treatments by bringing in targets is widely welcomed. But it falls short when it comes to talking therapies for teens and children, say experts.

Under new government targets due to take effect from next April in England, most people with depression who need talking therapies will begin treatment within six weeks, and A&E departments will be required to give suicidal patients the same priority as those with suspected heart attacks.

But while the new plan proposes that young people hit by psychosis for the first time should be seen within two weeks – the same target as for cancer patients – there is no promise of better access to talking therapies such as cognitive behavioural therapy for children and young people.

One in ten young will experience a mental health problem, according to the Office of National Statistics. Rates of mental health problems among children increase as they reach adolescence.

The new measures, described by Deputy Prime Minister Nick Clegg as the first step in reforming 'Cinderella' mental health services, have been widely welcomed.

Mark Winstanley, chief executive officer at Rethink Mental Illness, said: 'This is a watershed moment for everyone affected by mental illness and has the potential to improve the lives of millions.

'No one should have to wait months or even years for potentially life-changing treatment, just because they have a mental health problem rather than a physical one.'

Health professionals agree that action to improve mental health services is overdue. NHS Chief Executive Simon Stevens, writing in the foreword to the new five-year plan, described the disparity of mental health compared to physical health services as 'indefensible', leading to a treatment gap 'with most people with mental health problems receiving no treatment and with severe funding restrictions compared with physical health services'.

Three pupils in every class experience a mental health problem

In August, the government established a taskforce to look into the way mental health services for young people are delivered.

Sarah Brennan, chief executive of YoungMinds said on Wednesday the taskforce 'must ensure the recommendations it makes [due early next year] lead to major improvements in service provision, and are resourced in the same way as this announcement about adult services'.

In Oxfordshire a pioneering project is putting mental health professionals directly into schools. The idea is that young people in need of help can get it more easily, and with less disruption to their school lives, by having a mental health professional in school for half a day a week.

> **'It is absolutely unacceptable that we've got treatments we know work but we can't find ways to offer them'**
> **– Dr Mina Fazel**

Dr Mina Fazel, who is leading the project with Oxford Health NHS Trust, told Channel 4 News that the idea, which is based on successful initiatives in the United States, is more child-focused, and young people seem to like it: 'Schools end up managing a lot of pastoral care within the school system, and we have got to find ways to address this together.'

Paul James, headmaster of Cherwell school which has been running the new scheme since September, said: 'It is much easier for young people to get the help they need more quickly; while it is still early days for this approach, my colleagues report that it is already providing benefits for students who need this support.'

Oxfordshire is hoping to roll the scheme out to all 34 state-funded schools.

More than 75 per cent of adults who access mental health services had a diagnosable condition before the age of 18, so early treatment of young people could have a profound impact. As Dr Fazel told Channel 4 News: 'It is absolutely unacceptable that we've got treatments we know work but we can't find ways to offer them.'

8 October 2014

⇨ The above information is reprinted with kind permission from Channel 4 News. Please visit www.channel4.com for further information.

Stubbing out smoking can light up your mental health

Stopping smoking is associated with a significant improvement in mental health, equal to or larger than the effect from a course of anti-depressants, researchers at the University of Birmingham and Oxford have found.

The findings should give hope to those people who are desperate to quit smoking but rely on the vice as a stress reliever or anxiety buster.

And healthcare professionals who have been reluctant to offer smoking cessation advice to people with mental health disorders, for fear of quitting making them worse, should also be encouraged by the findings, which show that symptoms of depression, anxiety and stress are all reduced by stopping smoking.

The researchers carried out a review, published today (Friday) in the *BMJ*, of 26 studies looking at a wide range of mental health issues in people who stopped smoking. The results showed significant improvements in all mental health issues considered when people stopped smoking.

Although one explanation could be that people whose mental health improves for other reasons could be tempted to quit because they did not need to smoke to alleviate symptoms – but the inclusion of some studies in the review where all participants attempted to quit, regardless of their current mental health ruled this out.

The researchers were also able to rule out a deterioration in mental health as a reaction to failing to quit smoking, as some of the studies looked at people who were not motivated to stop in the first place – and would therefore not be adversely affected by continuing to smoke.

In addition, the reduction in mental health problems was equally evident for both the general population, and people who had already been diagnosed with mental health disorders, suggesting that clinicians should no longer be wary of intervening with smokers who have mental ill health.

The added mental health benefits of quitting smoking should also function as an added incentive for smokers to stop.

Gemma Taylor, the University of Birmingham researcher who led the study, said: 'It is hugely encouraging to be able to demonstrate that smoking cessation leads to an improvement in mental health. Smoking rates in the general population have declined substantially over the last 40 years. However, the rates of smoking in people with mental health problems have barely changed. Part of this disparity is due to the myth that stopping smoking will worsen mental health. I believe this research debunks this myth and I hope that these findings motivate people with and without mental health problems to stop smoking.'

Professor Paul Aveyard, from the University of Oxford, said: 'Patients often say to me 'doctor I'm too stressed to stop smoking now'. I hope doctors will now reassure those patients that there's a good chance that stopping smoking will make you less stressed. In fact, for people with chronic mental health problems, stopping smoking might be an effective treatment.'

14 February 2014

⇨ The above information is reprinted with kind permission from The University of Birmingham. Please visit www.bham.ac.uk for further information.

How drugs affect your mental health

Messing with brain chemicals is going to have consequences.

Drugs. We all know what they are and we have an idea why people take them, but do we know what the consequences for our mental health are?

Certain drugs (even prescription ones) can have a pretty big impact on your mental health, so it's a good idea to make sure you know the facts.

Psychoactive drugs

⇨ Heroin, cannabis, alcohol, ecstasy have a noticeable effect on your body but they're also going to have an impact on your mind.

⇨ They can create positive feelings in one person and negative feelings in another.

⇨ They can also create positive feelings in the short term, but bad ones in the long term.

What could they do to my mental health?

Well, for starters, they're going to interfere with the chemicals in your brain because that's what drugs do. That means your neurotransmitters (the chemicals that send messages through the brain) can't function properly.

One of the main reasons many people take drugs is because they believe they have a positive effect on their mood. However, you really need to ask yourself if the short-term buzz is worth the risk?

⇨ While some people talk of experiencing a high, others may have terrible panic attacks or drug-induced anxiety disorder. You could experience very severe anxiety with an increased heart rate, trembling, sweats, shortness of breath and a fear of losing control. You might also feel like your surroundings are strange and unreal, or that you are losing your personal identity and sense of reality.

⇨ Ever heard of psychosis? Well, you might go through a drug-induced psychosis, seeing and hearing things that aren't really there. Drug-induced delusions can also include smelling and tasting things that aren't there either.

⇨ Drug-induced mood disorder is another risk. You could feel incredibly depressed, sad, restless, irritable, tired or manic. An elevated mood, delusions, impulsive behaviour and racing thoughts may also be caused by drugs such as cocaine, amphetamines, heroin and methadone, to name a few.

⇨ If you're the kind of person who is prone to depression or has a family history of the condition, for example, alcohol or illegal drugs may not be the best thing to be introducing into your system. Ecstasy, for example, has an effect on the serotonin levels in your brain. That's the chemical which is thought to have a big impact on your mood and depression. If you take a lot of ecstasy over time your natural stores of serotonin may drop and you could end up with a lower level than you had originally. The less serotonin you have, the higher the risk of depression.

In some cases, psychoactive drugs can cause ongoing mental health conditions.

It's not clear why some people are affected and others aren't but it's thought that it might have something to do with the drugs triggering an underlying mental health condition or changing the way certain chemicals affect the brain.

For more information about drugs and the affect they can have on your mental health be sure to check out www.drugs.ie.

7 October 2014

⇨ The above information is reprinted with kind permission from SpunOut. Please visit www.spunout.ie for further information.

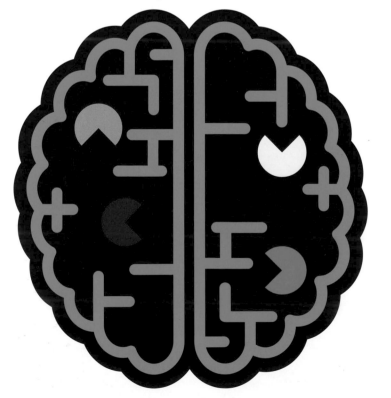

What is the relationship between sleep and mental health?

There is a close relationship between sleep and mental health. Many people who experience mental health problems also experience sleep problems.

Mental health problems that are often related to sleep problems include:

⇨ mood disorders, such as depression and bipolar disorder

⇨ anxiety disorders, such as anxiety, obsessive compulsive disorder (OCD) and social anxiety

⇨ psychotic disorders, such as schizophrenia.

How mental health problems can affect sleep

There are a number of different ways that a mental health problem can have an impact on your sleep. For example:

⇨ Stress and anxiety can cause you to have thoughts racing through your mind, making it difficult for you to sleep. If you are stressed or anxious you are also more likely to experience disturbed sleep, perhaps experiencing nightmares, sleep paralysis and sleep walking. If you have sleep problems over a long period of time, you may also develop anxiety or phobias about going to sleep, which can then cause insomnia or make existing insomnia worse.

⇨ Depression can mean that you find it very difficult to face your day-to-day responsibilities, and you may find yourself sleeping more in order to avoid them. This can lead to oversleeping – either sleeping late in the morning or a lot during the day. Oversleeping can cause fatigue and lethargy, and make it difficult to sleep well at night. If you experience difficult or troubling thoughts as part of depression, this can also cause insomnia. You may find it harder to fall asleep, or you may wake early and be unable to get back to sleep.

⇨ Post-traumatic stress disorder (PTSD) often causes nightmares and night terrors, forcing you to relive the situation that caused you trauma. This can cause disturbed sleep, and can lead you to feel anxious about falling asleep, which may then lead to insomnia.

⇨ Paranoia and psychosis can be extremely frightening, and may make it difficult for you to sleep. You may worry that something is going to happen to you or your family if you go to sleep – for example, that someone is going to break into your house or hurt a member of your family. You may hear voices or see things that you find frightening. Paranoia and psychosis can also lead to racing or disturbing thoughts, which can make it hard to relax and prevent you from falling asleep.

⇨ Mania often causes feelings of energy and elation. This may mean that you do not feel tired or do not want to sleep. Racing thoughts caused by mania can make it hard to fall asleep and may cause insomnia.

Psychiatric medications can cause sleep problems. Certain medications, such as antidepressants, can cause side effects that include insomnia, disturbed sleep or oversleeping. You may also have sleep problems after you have stopped taking psychiatric drugs. Some drugs may make physical causes of sleep problems worse – for example, benzodiazepines (a type of sleeping pill) can make existing sleep apnoea worse.

How sleep problems can affect mental health

Over a long period of time, a severe sleep problem could lead to a mental health problem, or may make an existing mental health problem worse.

Sleep problems can lead to any of the following:

⇨ Struggling to deal with everyday life – tiredness reduces your ability to deal with difficult situations as well as the challenges of day-to-day life. This may lower your self-esteem, make it harder to cope and cause your mental health to deteriorate.

⇨ Feeling of loneliness – fatigue can cause you to stop carrying out your usual social activities, leading you to become socially isolated. Social isolation can then lead to mental health problems such as depression or anxiety.

⇨ Low mood – if you don't get enough sleep, or if your sleep is disturbed, this can affect your mood, energy levels and ability to cope with daily tasks. If this occurs over a long period of time, it can start to have an effect on your mental health, and lead to mental health problems, such as depression or anxiety.

⇨ Negative thoughts – if you are tired, this can affect your ability to rationalise anxieties and irrational thoughts, which can feed into negative thinking patterns associated with mental health problems.

⇨ Psychotic episodes – if you have a psychotic disorder, or bipolar disorder, a lack of sleep can trigger mania, psychosis and paranoia, or make existing symptoms worse.

⇨ The above information is reprinted with kind permission from Mind. Please visit www.mind.org.uk for further information.

GPs to be given £55 for every diagnosis of dementia

GPs are to be given £55 for every patient they diagnose with dementia under new plans from NHS England.

The new scheme forms part of a £5 million funding boost for general practice, announced by NHS chief executive Simon Stevens at the Royal College of General Practitioners conference earlier this month.

The service is optional for GPs to take part in and bases payment on the net increase in the dementia register at the end of March 2015, compared with the end of September 2014.

This move is part of NHS England's ongoing push to identify and diagnose two-thirds of people with dementia by April 2015.

George McNamara, Head of Policy and Public Affairs at the Alzheimer's Society said:

'Given that only half of people living with dementia receive a diagnosis, any steps towards improving diagnosis is a good thing. However, a focus on enhanced payments is only part of the answer and alone will not suffice.

'GPs are motivated by caring for their patients, not ticking boxes. We know that some doctors are reluctant to give a diagnosis because they know the right help and support isn't available locally. It's absolutely vital that every person with dementia understands what is happening to them and has access to the help they need afterwards.

'The Alzheimer's Society will be working closely with CCGs and GP practices to support them in reaching out to people worried about their memory.'

22 October 2014

⇨ The above information is reprinted with kind permission from the Alzheimer's Society. Please visit www.alzheimers.org.uk for further information.

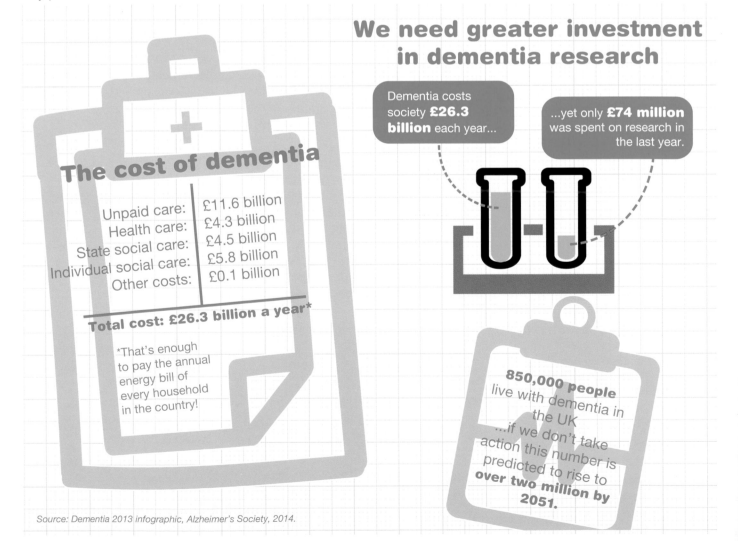

The cost of dementia

Unpaid care:	£11.6 billion
Health care:	£4.3 billion
State social care:	£4.5 billion
Individual social care:	£5.8 billion
Other costs:	£0.1 billion

Total cost: £26.3 billion a year*

*That's enough to pay the annual energy bill of every household in the country!

We need greater investment in dementia research

Dementia costs society **£26.3 billion** each year...

...yet only **£74 million** was spent on research in the last year.

850,000 people live with dementia in the UK ...if we don't take action this number is predicted to rise to **over two million by 2051.**

Source: Dementia 2013 infographic, Alzheimer's Society, 2014.

The future of mental health services

Mental health services must act to avoid sleepwalking into the future.

A report, published today by the Mental Health Foundation sets out some key messages as to what mental health services need to do in order to ensure that they are ready to address the mental health needs of the UK population in 20–30 years' time.

The year-long Inquiry into the future of mental health services was co-chaired by Professor Dinesh Bhugra from the Institute of Psychiatry at King's College London.

Mental health services are currently straining at the seams. Yet they face even greater pressures in the future, including a growing, and ageing, population; persistently high prevalence rates of mental disorders among adults and children; increasing levels of co-morbid mental and physical health problems; and funding constraints that are likely to last for many years.

⇨ Mental illness causes immense distress to millions of people across the UK and their families, with an annual cost of over £100 billion to the economy.

⇨ If prevalence rates for mental disorders do not fall, by 2030 there will be two million more adults and 100,000 more children with mental health problems in the UK than there are today.

⇨ Mental Health Foundation inquiry identifies the significant challenges that mental health services must address in order to be fit for purpose for 21st century.

Professor Dinesh Bhugra, from the Institute of Psychiatry at King's College London and co-chair of the Inquiry Advisory Panel for the Mental Health Foundation, said: 'A range of factors will undoubtedly impact on future mental health services such as a larger population with more people reaching later life and increased expectations of care and support.

'We need to start taking action today to address future challenges. We cannot expect mental health services simply to muddle along with no clear sense of what is required, and sleepwalk into the future. If we do so, we will be failing all those who in the future need mental health care and their families, as well as the staff who work in mental health services.

'Our inquiry found that the case for more preventative work is undeniable. Lacking a "cure" for mental illness, a reduction in the number of people across the UK developing mental disorders appears to us to be the only way that mental health services will adequately cope with demand in 20–30 years' time.

'We need fresh ways of working in mental health, ensuring the best use of available resources and working in truly integrated fashion. New technology will no doubt bring about more changes as well as challenges. But much of what in our view needs to be done is simply implementing known good practice that already exists. Failure to provide good, integrated mental health care is not a failure of understanding what needs to be done, it is a failure of actually implementing good practice in organisational strategies and the day to-day business of providing people with the care and treatment that they want. We need to start today to rectify that.'

Key findings:

The Inquiry looked at certain key demographic and societal factors which will impact on future mental health services and identified six key themes that mental health services will need to address to become fit for purpose for the 21st century:

1. Personalising services

Greater personalisation of services and the engagement of patients and their carers and families as equal partners in decisions about care and service provision.

2. Integrated care

Increased integration driven by committed local leaders between different parts of mental health services; between physical and mental health care; and between health and social care. This will need a new approach to training health and social care staff, and a change in culture and attitudes.

3. Life span issues

Services that are designed to address an individual's mental health, and mental health needs, across the life span from infancy to old age.

4. Workforce development

Shared training across disciplines from the start of people's careers and in continuing professional development, moving psychiatry into community and primary care settings, and flexibility for staff to develop and move careers across disciplines.

5. Research and new technologies

Better funded research, into both clinical and social interventions to support people with mental health problems, alongside a commitment to ensure equality of access to the benefits of new technologies.

6. Public mental health

A need for mental health to be treated as a core public health issue, so that it will be as normal for everyone to look after their mental health as it is to look after their physical health and a public health workforce that sees mental health as one of its core responsibilities.

23 September 2013

⇨ The above information is reprinted with kind permission from King's College London. Please visit www.kcl.ac.uk for further information.

Mental health of children and young people 'at risk in digital age'

Cyberbullying and rise in self-harm highlighted by MPs voicing concern over violent video games and sexting.

By Denis Campbell, health correspondent

Violent video games, the sharing of indecent images on mobile phones, and other types of digital communications, are harming young people's mental health, MPs warned on Wednesday, amid evidence of big increases in self-harm and serious psychological problems among the under-18s.

Cyberbullying and websites advocating anorexia and self-harm are also posing a danger to the mental well-being of children and young people, the Commons Health Select Committee says in its report.

Sarah Wollaston, chair of the Committee, who was a GP for 24 years before becoming a Tory MP in 2010, said: 'In the past if you were being bullied it might just be in the classroom. Now it follows [you] way beyond the walk home from school. It is there all the time. Voluntary bodies have not suggested stopping young people using the Internet. But for some young people it's clearly a new source of stress.'

However, the MPs said they had found no evidence that the emerging digital culture was behind the worrying rise, of up to 25% to 30% a year, in numbers of children and young people seeking treatment for mental health problems.

The cross-party group acknowledges that forms of online and social communication are now central to the lives of under-18s, but says that a government inquiry into the effects is needed because of the potential for harm.

'For today's children and young people, digital culture and social media are an integral part of life... this has the potential to significantly increase stress and to amplify the effects of bullying,' the Committee's report says.

Some young people experience 'bullying, harassment and threats of violence' when online, the MPs say. While they did not look into Internet regulation in depth during their six-month inquiry, they concluded: 'In our view sufficient concern has been raised to warrant a more detailed consideration of the impact of the Internet on children's and young people's mental health, and in particular the use of social media and impact of pro-anorexia, self-harm and other inappropriate websites.'

It calls on the Department of Health and NHS England's joint taskforce, now investigating, alongside bodies such as the UK Council for Child Internet Safety, the mental health of under-18s, to assess the impact of social media.

The MPs appreciate the move for e-safety to be taught at all four education key-stages in England. But they also want the Department for Education, as part of a review of mental health education in schools, to 'ensure that links between online safety, cyberbullying, and maintaining and protecting emotional well-being and mental health are fully articulated'.

Wollaston voiced concern that 'sexting' (sharing indecent photographs) could be traumatic for vulnerable young women persuaded to pose for intimate pictures then finding the shots shared widely. Some would end up being harassed, she said. Sexting had 'become normalised in some school environments', she said. 'We need much better education about the dangers of sexting.' She also expressed unease about the impact of violent video games played by young people. Parents, she said, should do more to check what their offspring were doing online in their free time and talk to them because 'if they are spending two hours a night doing that, is that harming their child?'

Lucie Russell, director of campaigns and media at the charity Young Minds, said: 'The 24/7 online world has the potential to massively increase young people's stress levels and multiplies the opportunities for them to connect with others in similar distress. Websites like Tumblr, where there has been recent media focus on self-harm blogs, must do all they can to limit triggering content and that which encourages self-harming behaviour.'

Russell backed the committee's view that the Internet could also be 'a valuable source of support for children and young people with mental health problems'. But, she added that 'many professionals feel completely out of touch with, even intimidated by, social media and the net'.

The report paints a grim picture of the growing number of under-18s needing

care, often struggling to access it, or becoming an inpatient hundreds of miles from home, as children's and adolescents' mental health services tried to cope with budget cuts, lack of staff and too few beds.

'Major problems' in accessing services ends with 'children and young people's safety being compromised while they wait for a bed to become available', say the MPs.

Services are under such pressure that in some parts of England children only get seen by a psychiatrist if they have already tried to take their own lives at least once.

Despite growing need, criteria for being referred for NHS treatment have been tightened in most of England, the MPs say.

Liz Myers, a consultant psychiatrist with the Cornwall Partnership NHS foundation trust, told the inquiry that its services for the young were receiving 4,000 referrals a year, though were only commissioned by the NHS to do 2,000.

'This has meant that we are necessarily having to prioritise those who have the most urgent and pressing need, and we have no capacity for earlier intervention and very little capacity for seeing those perhaps with the less life-threatening or urgent risky presentations.

'There are increasing waits. It is not okay. We do not want that for our children and young people, but we have to just keep prioritising.'

Hilary Cass, president of the Royal College of Paediatrics and Child Health, said failure to tackle emerging problems with young people's mental health meant the issue was now 'a hidden epidemic'.

5 November 2014

⇨ The above information is reprinted with kind permission from *The Guardian*. Please visit www.theguardian.com for further information.

Are young people turning to social media for mental health support?

Young people who are experiencing mental health problems are increasingly turning to the Internet and social media for support, instead of parents or healthcare professionals, writes Lauren Blenkinsop.

YOUNGMINDS
The voice for young people's **mental health and wellbeing**

A recent article by Mindswork states:

'The Internet is both a one-stop shop and a social hang out. Whether a young person is going there to find out about the War of the Roses for A-Level History or to understand why they or a friend might be self-harming, chances are they go there before anything else.'

This is supported by recent research carried out by YoungMinds and Cello, which showed that in the instance of self-harm, 73% of young people relied on TV, radio, social networks and websites to get information. This is compared to just 11% who sought information from healthcare professionals. Interestingly, 50% of the young people questioned felt they should be talking to their parents about it, but only 10% felt comfortable doing so. These statistics demonstrate that although young people are getting the message about talking to people about mental health problems, in reality they find it much easier to shelter in the anonymity of the Internet and seek help online.

Blogging sites such as Tumblr make it very easy to find and share personal experiences, whether it is worries about self-harm, issues with body image, reviews of medication or anything else.

Many young people are turning to blogging sites to discuss their struggles with mental health issues, and as a result these sites have become something of an unofficial resource of mental health information, as people looking for information read through various personal accounts. Sharing experiences can often be a very positive thing; however, if personal accounts are the only source of information someone seeking advice has available to them the picture can be distorted, as everybody's experiences of mental health problems are different. For example, one person's account of having a bad experience on one type of medication should not be used as a reason to avoid that particular drug, and should never replace going to a doctor to discuss medication.

There is also the risk when seeking help online that you come across sites and blogs that are in fact detrimental. There are many blogs and images on the Internet that glorify problems such as self-harm and eating disorders, and these pose a real threat to young people, particularly if they are already struggling with a mental health problem. This is why it is vital that there are easily accessible online resources that offer accurate and supportive information for young people.

Popular online comics such as 'Hyperbole and a Half' and 'Robot Hugs' try to counteract these detrimental messages with honest representations of mental health, as well as advice for dealing with these problems. Their images spread through social networking sites like wildfire and are reposted to hundreds of thousands of Twitter accounts, blogs and Facebook profiles as they offer a funny but accurate portrayal of living with anxiety and depression. Their popularity lies in their instant accessibility, and finding blogs such as these can be a source of comfort as it shows that you are not alone in your experiences. They do not, however, offer important medical information, an issue that a new initiative from YoungMinds seeks to address. In March 2014, YoungMinds launched headmeds.org.uk, a website offering easily accessible information on mental health medication for young people. YoungMinds' Online Communications Editor, Tamsin Fidgeon says:

'There is a plethora of information on mental health medication out there. However, there is nothing specifically for young people, answering the difficult questions that they may have such as, "Will this medication affect my sex life?", or "Can I smoke weed while taking these meds?". This is vital information that young people have told us they want to know, yet many do not feel comfortable asking these questions at the time of diagnosis or to the GP who treats their parents too. Young people obtain much of their information online and HeadMeds provides answers in an accessible way, detailed information about the possible side effects that a young person may get as a result of taking some medications, and how common those side effects are.'

When young people are saying that they find Google to be their 'most comfortable source of information', it is important that mental health resources adapt to meet the new online generation's needs. Hopefully, sites such as "HeadMeds" will be able to meet this need. Until then, it is important to recognise that social media has become a key resource for young people, but that it cannot be a substitute for specialised support.

November 2014

⇨ The above information is reprinted with kind permission from YoungMinds. Please visit www.youngminds.org.uk for further information.

Five steps to mental well-being

Scientific evidence points to five steps that we can take to improve our mental well-being. If you give them a try, you may feel happier, more positive and able to get the most from your life.

Your mental health is important. Some mental illnesses, such as depression and anxiety, are common. If you have such an illness, it's important to get the right treatment.

However, there's more to good mental health than avoiding or treating mental illness. There is also positive mental well-being.

Why is mental well-being important? First, we all want to feel good about ourselves and the world around us, and be able to get the most from our lives.

There is also evidence that good mental well-being is important for our physical health, and that it can help us achieve the goals we set for ourselves.

What is mental well-being?

Sarah Stewart-Brown, professor of public health at the University of Warwick and a well-being expert, says that when we talk about mental well-being, we mean more than just happiness.

'It's useful to start with the idea that overall well-being involves both the mind and the body. And we know that physical and mental well-being are closely related,' she says.

'Of course, feeling happy is a part of mental well-being. But it is far from the whole. There is a deeper kind of well-being, which is about living in a way that is good for you and good for others around you.

'Feelings of contentment, enjoyment, confidence and engagement with the world are all a part of mental well-being. Self-esteem and self-confidence are, too. So is a feeling that you can do the things you want to do. And so are good relationships, which bring joy to you and those around you.

'Of course, good mental well-being does not mean that you never experience feelings or situations that you find difficult. But it does mean that you feel you have the resilience to cope when times are tougher than usual.'

Mental well-being can take many different forms, but a useful description is feeling good and functioning well.

Well-being and society

Over the last 50 years, we in Britain have become richer. Despite this, evidence from population surveys – in which people were asked to rate their own happiness or mental well-being – shows that mental well-being has not improved.

This suggests that many of the things we often think will improve our mental well-being – such as more possessions, more money to spend or expensive holidays – on their own do not lead to a lasting improvement in the way we feel about ourselves and our lives.

The message is clear: it's time to rethink well-being.

Evidence and well-being

Over the last 20 years, new evidence has emerged about what really causes lasting improvements to mental well-being.

'Some of this evidence comes from observational studies in which scientists look at the behaviour and well-being of certain sections of the population,' says Professor Stewart-Brown. 'Other evidence comes from trials in which scientists take a group of people and ask them to change their behaviour or participate in a treatment or other intervention, such as an exercise programme, and then watch what happens to their well-being.'

To gain evidence on well-being, scientists have to find ways to measure it. Often, they measure well-being using a series of questions that ask subjects how they feel about themselves, their lives and the world around them.

Well-being in your life

Many factors influence our well-being. Evidence shows that the actions we take and the way we think have the biggest impact.

It can help to think about 'being well' as something you do, rather than something you are. The more you put in, the more you are likely to get out.

'The first thing you can do for your own well-being is become curious about it,' says Professor Stewart-Brown.

'Start to think about what you've done in the past to promote mental well-being, and whether it worked. Then think about new things that you can try.

'Remember, no-one can give well-being to you. It's you who has to take action.'

Five steps to mental well-being

Evidence suggests there are five steps we can all take to improve our mental well-being.

If you approach them with an open mind and try them out, you can judge the results yourself.

⇨ connect – connect with the people around you: your family, friends, colleagues and neighbours. Spend time developing these relationships.

⇨ be active – you don't have to go to the gym. Take a walk, go cycling or play a game of football. Find the activity that you enjoy and make it a part of your life.

⇨ keep learning – learning new skills can give you a sense of achievement and a new confidence. So why not sign up for that cooking course, start learning to play a musical instrument, or figure out how to fix your bike?

⇨ give to others – even the smallest act can count, whether it's a smile, a thank you or a kind word. Larger acts, such as volunteering at your local community centre, can improve your mental well-being and help you build new social networks.

⇨ take notice – be more aware of the present moment, including your feelings and thoughts, your body and the world around you. Some people call this awareness 'mindfulness', and it can positively change the way you feel about life and how you approach challenges.

6 January 2014

⇨ The above information is reprinted with kind permission from NHS Choices. Please visit www.nhs.uk for further information.

First aid classes offered in mental health

By Liz Lockhart

A mental health board in Illinois, America, is offering a 12-hour mental health first aid class spread over three days, starting on Friday 7 June.

This will be a continuing education class which offers information on how to recognise and assist someone who might be in the early stages of distress. It is aimed at helping someone who is developing a mental health problem or who is in mental health turmoil.

The class teaches signs and symptoms of differing mental health disorders and also demonstrates effective response to individuals showing symptoms.

In a news release the Mental Health Board officials said 'Mental health first aid is comparable to first aid for physical problems. It teaches important skills and helps to reduce the stigma associated with mental illness.'

'The general lack of knowledge about mental health problems adds to the stigma that might prevent people from seeking help, and it prevents people from providing support.' the release said.

'Mental health first aid is a public education programme designed for community groups, law enforcement and other emergency responders, school staff, businesses and the pubic so that they can identify, understand and respond to signs of mental illness.' Wendy Neuman, programme monitor and training assistant for the Mental Health Board said.

'Mental health problems are very common, with the most common being depression, anxiety disorders and psychotic disorders,' Neuman said. 'Frequently, substance abuse is a co-occurring problem.'

One in every four adults is affected by a diagnosable mental illness in any given year according to the National Institute of Mental Health. They explain that this class is to teach participants about the symptoms, possible risk factors and where and how to get help. It also teaches tips on how to deal with people whose illness makes them irrational. Basic skills are taught as a bridge until professional help can be found.

'Education reduces people's fear of the unknown,' Neuman said.

What a great idea – let's hope it can be rolled out across the planet.

2013

⇨ The above information is reprinted with kind permission from Mental Healthy. Please visit www. mentalhealthy.co.uk for further information.

Mindfulness

Do you allow your thoughts and feelings to get the better of you? Do you sometimes find it difficult to cope with everyday pressures? Well, you're not alone.

Difficult or stressful situations can leave you feeling sad, anxious or angry. And these emotions can make you feel like you're no longer in control and are unable to cope with the situation.

But help may be at hand. 'Mindfulness' could help you change the way you think, feel and act.

What is mindfulness?

Put simply, mindfulness is a mind-body based training that uses meditation, breathing and yoga techniques to help you focus on your thoughts and feelings. Mindfulness helps you manage your thoughts and feelings better, instead of being overwhelmed by them.

FACT: Mindfulness meditation can help you improve your performance at work and relationships at home.

How does mindfulness work?

Mindfulness therapy encourages you to change the way you think, feel and act. You learn techniques to help you become more aware of how you respond to stressful situations. Paying attention to the way you think and feel about your experiences means you can learn to break your negative thought patterns. It helps you change the way you behave by building up positive thoughts and ways to deal with different situations.

FACT: Your physical and mental well-being is affected by the way you think and the way you handle your feelings.

What are the benefits of mindfulness?

Mindfulness meditation enables you to deal with thoughts and emotions in everyday life in a more balanced way. When practised regularly, it can help improve your health and well-being.

Research has shown that mindfulness meditation improves concentration, reduces feelings of stress and anxiety, and can help you take better control of addictive behaviour. Mindfulness can even have a positive effect on physical problems such as high blood pressure, heart disease and chronic pain.

If you have bouts of depression, a treatment called mindfulness-based cognitive therapy can help reduce your chances of becoming depressed again. It combines mindfulness techniques with elements from cognitive behavioural therapy (CBT) to help break negative thought patterns.

FACT: Many health professionals believe mindfulness meditation would be helpful for people with mental health problems.

Being mindful

Being mindful means learning to live in the present. This means being more fully aware of what is around you – what you can see, hear, touch and taste. It's also about being aware of your thoughts and feelings as they are happening. People often find mindfulness harder to do than it sounds. But once you've learnt the basic techniques, you can use them whenever you need to calm yourself or refocus your energy and attention. Here are some activities to help you focus on the present moment.

⇨ Close your eyes and observe what you see in your mind.

⇨ Observe and describe an object in the room.

⇨ Observe taste and sensation while eating a strawberry

⇨ Observe your thoughts and emotions that you experience when listening to a particular poem or music.

Want to learn more?

Mindfulness is becoming better known and more practised. There are courses and classes that can help you learn more about it. For more information about mindfulness speak to your doctor or take a look at the Resources section below.

Resources

Further information

⇨ Mental Health Foundation

  • www.mentalhealth.org.uk

⇨ Oxford Mindfulness Centre

  • www.oxfordmindfulness.org

Sources

⇨ Mindfulness. Mental Health Foundation. www.mentalhealth.org.uk, accessed 15 July 2013

⇨ About mindfulness. Mental Health Foundation. www.bemindful.co.uk, accessed 15 July 2013

⇨ Find a course near you. Mental Health Foundation. www.bemindful.co.uk, accessed 15 July 2013

⇨ Williams JMG, Kuyken W. Mindfulness-based cognitive therapy: a promising new approach to preventing depressive relapse. *The British Journal of Psychiatry* 2012; 200:359–360. doi:10.1192/bjp.bp.111.104745.

⇨ About mindfulness. Oxford Mindfulness Centre. www.oxfordmindfulness.org, accessed 15 July 2013

⇨ Mindfulness activities. The Minnesota Association of Community Mental Health Programs. www.macmhp.org, accessed 15 July 2013

⇨ Bring mindfulness into your day. Action for Happiness. www.actionforhappiness.org, accessed 18 July 2013

⇨ The above information is reprinted with kind permission from BUPA. Please visit www.bupa.co.uk for further information.

CBT: therapy worth talking about

What is CBT?

CBT, or Cognitive Behaviour Therapy, is a talking therapy. It has been proved to help treat a wide range of emotional and physical health conditions in adults, young people and children. CBT looks at how we think about a situation and how this affects the way we act. In turn our actions can affect how we think and feel. The therapist and client work together in changing the client's behaviours, or their thinking patterns, or both of these.

CBT works

There is a great deal of research evidence to show that CBT works effectively in treating depression. This research has been carefully reviewed by the National Institute for Health and Clinical Excellence (NICE).

NICE provides independent, evidence-based guidance for the NHS on the most effective ways to treat disease and ill health. CBT is recommended by NICE for the treatment of anxiety disorders.

What can CBT help with?

NICE recommends CBT in the treatment of the following conditions:

⇨ anxiety disorders (including panic attacks and post-traumatic stress disorder)

⇨ depression

⇨ obsessive compulsive disorder

⇨ schizophrenia and psychosis

⇨ bipolar disorder.

There is also good evidence that CBT is helpful in treating many other conditions, including:

⇨ chronic fatigue

⇨ behavioural difficulties in children

⇨ anxiety disorders in children

⇨ chronic pain

⇨ physical symptoms without a medical diagnosis

⇨ sleep difficulties

⇨ anger management.

CBT can be used if you are on medication which has been prescribed by your GP. You can also use CBT on its own. This will depend on the difficulty you want help with.

How CBT is delivered

CBT can be offered in individual sessions with a therapist or as part of a group. The number of CBT sessions you need depends on the difficulty you need help with. Often this will be between five and 20 weekly sessions lasting between 30 and 60 minutes each. CBT is mainly concerned with how you think and act now, instead of looking at and getting help with difficulties in your past.

You and your therapist will discuss your specific difficulties and set goals for you to achieve. CBT is not a quick fix. It involves hard work during and between sessions. Your therapist will not tell you what to do. Instead they will help you decide what difficulties you want to work on in order to help you improve your situation. Your therapist will be able to advise you on how to continue using CBT techniques in your daily life after your treatment ends.

CBT is available in a wide range of settings, as well as hospitals or clinics. It is sometimes provided in the form of written or computer-based packages. This may be combined with flexible telephone or face-to-face appointments to check progress and help overcome any barriers to putting into practice what you have learned. This way of delivering CBT has made it more accessible to people with busy lives, and has also reduced delays in getting help.

Self-help CBT

CBT-based self-help books are available. There are also websites providing information on CBT techniques which are free to access. Evidence does show that using them works better with support from a therapist, especially for low mood.

Finding a therapist

CBT is now widely available on the NHS for the treatment of depression. If you feel that CBT may be helpful, then you should first discuss it with your GP. Private therapists are also available. Before starting CBT, it is recommended that you check that your therapist is accredited by BABCP. You can find details of all CBT therapists accredited by BABCP online at www.cbtregisteruk.com.

About BABCP

BABCP stands for the British Association for Behavioural & Cognitive Psychotherapies. It has been the lead organisation for CBT in the UK since 1972. BABCP members work in the NHS, social care, education and universities. BABCP also provides accreditation to those who practise CBT in the NHS and privately. It is widely recognised by health and social care employers, training institutions and health insurance companies. BABCP believes that accreditation is important in protecting the public and raising the quality of CBT.

Published October 2012

⇨ The above information is reprinted with kind permission from the British Association for Behavioural & Cognitive Psychotherapies (BABCP). Please visit www.babcp.com for further information.

Key facts

- More than 2,000 viewers were questioned and more than half (54%) stated that seeing a well-known character on screen portrayed as having a mental health problem improved their understanding of what it involved. (page 2)

- Inclusions and removals in the *Diagnostic and Statistical Manual of Mental Disorders* can be hugely controversial. Autism is in the manual, for example, but Asperger's isn't. Homosexuality was only removed in 1974. (page 3)

- One in four people will experience a mental health problem in any given year. (page 5)

- People with a mental illness are more likely to be a victim of violence. (page 5)

- Nine out of ten people with mental health problems experience stigma and discrimination. (page 5)

- Nearly three in four young people fear the reactions of friends when they talk about their mental health problems. (page 5)

- Over a three-month, 63% of references to mental health in TV soaps and drama were 'pejorative, flippant or unsympathetic' terms and included: 'crackpot', 'a sad little psycho', 'basket case', 'where did you get her from?', 'Care in the Community?' and 'he was looney tunes'. (page 5)

- After adjusting for age, men in the lowest household income group were three times more likely to have a common mental disorder than those in the highest income households (23.5 per cent and 8.8 per cent, respectively). (page 6)

- In the reporting year 2012/13, there were 50,408 detentions under the Mental Health Act. This is four per cent (1,777) greater than during the 2011/12 reporting period. (page 7)

- Homeless Link estimates that around 70 per cent of people accessing homelessness services have a mental health problem. (page 8)

- Half of all mental disorder first emerges before the age of 14 years and three quarters by age 25 years. (page 10)

- If one of your biological parents has bipolar disorder, there is a 15 in 100 chance of it being passed down to you. If both of your biological parents have bipolar disorder, there is a 50 in 100 chance of it being passed down to you. (page 12)

- 42% think that the amount of money the Government currently spends on providing services to the mentally ill is too low. 21% think it is about right, 7% think it is too high and 30% are not sure. (page 14)

- The mental health trust budget rose to its highest in 2011/12 but referrals also rose by 13%. Last year's budget fell by 2.3%, despite higher demand. (page 16)

- It costs £13 a day to support someone with psychosis or schizophrenia in the community. If they were to stay in hospital it would cost £350 a day. (page 16)

- Combat Stress charity reports 57% increase in number of ex-military personnel needing treatment in 2013 and says UK must prepare for escalation. (page 18)

- Research shows that FTSE 100 companies that prioritise employee engagement and well-being outperform the rest of the FTSE 100 by 10%. (page 19)

- Scottish Trades Union Congress (STUC) reported that on average employees take 21 days for each period of absence related to mental health. (page 19)

- One in six workers will experience a mental health problem. (page 20)

- 40% of British employers would hire someone with a mental health condition. (page 20)

- Data published yesterday by the Health and Social Care Information Centre (HSCIC) shows that between April and November 2013, 250 under-18s were recorded as spending time on adult mental health wards. (page 22)

- GPs are to be given £55 for every patient they diagnose with dementia under new plans from NHS England. (page32)

- Mental illness causes immense distress to millions of people across the UK and their families, with an annual cost of over £100 billion to the economy. (page 33)

- If prevalence rates for mental disorders do not fall, by 2030 there will be two million more adults and 100,000 more children with mental health problems in the UK than there are today. (page 33)

- Recent research carried out by YoungMinds and Cello, which showed that in the instance of self-harm, 73% of young people relied on TV, radio, social networks and websites to get information. (page 35)

Alzheimer's disease

A progressive form of dementia involving deterioration of the brain tissue. Alzheimer's patients suffer from memory loss, confusion, mood swings and personality changes. Most often, it is diagnosed in elderly people, although the rarer early-onset Alzheimer's can occur much earlier. Alzheimer's disease is a terminal illness for which there is no cure.

Anxiety

Anxiety can be described as a feeling of fear, apprehension, tension and/or stress. Most people experience anxiety from time to time and this is a perfectly normal response to stress. However, some individuals suffer from anxiety disorders which cause them to experience symptoms such as intense, persistent fear or nervousness, panic attacks and hyperventilation.

Bipolar disorder

Previously called manic depression, this illness is characterised by mood swings where periods of severe depression are balanced by periods of elation and overactivity (mania).

Cognitive behavioural therapy (CBT)

A psychological treatment which assumes that behavioural and emotional reactions are learned over a long period. A cognitive therapist will seek to identify the source of emotional problems and develop techniques to overcome them.

Dementia

Mental deterioration and a reduction in brain function caused by loss of brain cells. Alzheimer's disease is the most common form of dementia.

Depression

Someone is said to be significantly depressed, or suffering from depression, when feelings of sadness or misery don't go away quickly and are so bad that they interfere with everyday life. Symptoms can also include low self-esteem and a lack of motivation.

Diagnostic and Statistical Manual of Mental Disorders (DSM)

This is a manual used by clinicians, researchers, pharmaceutical companies, the legal system and many more which provides a standard set of criteria to classify mental disorders. It is currently in its fifth edition which was published on 18 May 2013.

Mental health/well-being

Everyone has 'mental health' and this can be thought of in terms of: how we feel about ourselves and the people around us, our ability to make and keep friends and relationships, our ability to learn from others and to develop psychologically and emotionally and also about having the strength to overcome the difficulties and challenges we can all face at times in our lives – to have confidence and self-esteem.

Mental Health Act 1983

If someone has been 'sectioned' (or 'detained') under the Mental Health Act 1983, this means that an individual has been suffering from mental health issues and has been taken from a public place to a 'place of safety' for their protection, and so they can be medically assessed – this is done without their agreement, but ultimately for their own safety.

Mindfulness

Mind-body based training that uses meditation, breathing and yoga techniques to help you focus on your thoughts and feelings. Mindfulness helps you manage your thoughts and feelings better, instead of being overwhelmed by them.

Post-Traumatic Stress Disorder (PTSD)

PTSD is a psychological response to an intensely traumatic event. It is commonly observed in members of the armed forces and has been known by different names at different times in history: during the First World War, for example, it was known as 'shell shock'.

Psychiatrist

A medical doctor who specialises in diagnosing and treating mental disorders. This is different from a psychologist, who is a professional or academic (not necessarily a doctor) specialising in understanding the human mind, thought and human behaviour.

Psychosis

A mental state in which the perception of reality is distorted.

Schizophrenia

Disorder characterised by hallucinations, paranoid delusions and abnormal thought patterns.

Assignments

Brainstorming

⇨ In small groups, discuss what you know about mental health and mental illness. Consider the following points:

- What is mental health?

- What is the Mental Health Act 1983?

- Which mental illness are you aware of? Write down a list and compare it with a partner.

Research

⇨ Visit some online newspaper archives and carry out a search for articles which refer to mental illness. Choose three relevant articles from three different newspapers and analyse the language and terminology they use in discussing mental health. Do the papers vary in their attitude and tone? Based on your research, do you think the media perpetuates the stigma attached to mental illness or discourages it? Write some notes and feedback to your class.

⇨ Visit Mind's website: www.mind.org.uk. What are the aims of this organisation? What support do they offer for people suffering from mental health problems? Write a short review of the site, including how accessible you feel the information is and how easy you find the site to use.

⇨ Research mental health charities and support groups in your local area and then think about how you might promote them in your community. Write some notes and feedback to your class.

Design

⇨ Read the article *Five new mental disorders you could have under DSM-5* on page 3. Choose one of the lesser known mental disorders and design a poster to help raise awareness for this condition.

⇨ Create a leaflet that helps bust the myths surrounding mental illness. You might find the article *Mental health statistics, facts and myths* on page 5 helpful.

⇨ Choose one of the articles in this book and create an illustration to highlight the key themes/message of your chosen article.

⇨ Design a website that will give parents information about mental well-being in young people. Think about the kind of information they might need and give your site a name and logo.

⇨ Design an app that, in some way, will help people suffering from mental illness. Think carefully about what your app will do and what problem it will address. Think of a name and produce some sketches or written ideas for content. You can undertake this assignment individually or in pairs.

Oral

⇨ Role-play a situation in which one of you is an employer looking to fill a vacancy within your company and the other is someone applying for the job who is well qualified for the job but suffers from a mental illness, such as bipolar disorder. Put yourself in that person's position and think carefully about what kind of questions and concerns you might have. Take it in turns to play the role of the employer and the job-seeker.

⇨ 'Violent video games, the sharing of indecent images on mobile phones, and other types of digital communications, are harming young people's mental health.' Debate this motion as a class, with one group arguing in favour and the other against.

Reading/writing

⇨ Write a diary entry from the point of view of someone who suffers from a mental illness such as depression. Imagine how they would feel and what challenges they could face in their day-to-day life. You may need to do further research into the mental illness you have chosen.

⇨ Read the article *Nick Clegg announces NHS to put mental health issues on same footing as cancer* (pages 26-27) and write a summary for your school newspaper.

⇨ Read *The Silver Linings Playbook* by Matthew Quick and write an essay discussing how the author deals with the subject of mental illness. Do you think he addresses the stigma surrounding mental illness? Did the book affect your attitude towards people who suffer from or mental ill health? Write no more than 1,500 words.

⇨ Write a one-paragraph definition of cognitive behavioural therapy.

⇨ Write a blog post from the point of view of a young person suffering from a mental illness. Explore your feelings about your illness, considering who you might talk to and where you might turn for help.

⇨ Read the article *Police custody is regularly being used to detain people whose only 'crime' is that they are suffering from a mental disorder, a joint inspection has found* on page 24 and rewrite a summary for your school newspaper.

⇨ Is there a difference between mental health and mental illness? Write a one-page essay exploring your thoughts.

Acknowledgements

The publisher is grateful for permission to reproduce the material in this book. While every care has been taken to trace and acknowledge copyright, the publisher tenders its apology for any accidental infringement or where copyright has proved untraceable. The publisher would be pleased to come to a suitable arrangement in any such case with the rightful owner.

Images

All images courtesy of iStock, except page 15: MorgueFile, page 24 © My_Southborough, page 32: icons from Freepik.

Illustrations

Don Hatcher: pages 3 & 10. Simon Kneebone: pages 13 & 25. Angelo Madrid: pages 16 & 27.

Additional acknowledgements

Editorial on behalf of Independence Educational Publishers by Cara Acred.

With thanks to the Independence team: Mary Chapman, Sandra Dennis, Christina Hughes, Jackie Staines and Jan Sunderland.

Cara Acred

Cambridge

January 2015

Contents

26111

26111

Introduction

Discussing Sexual Health is Volume 237 in the *ISSUES* series. The aim of the series is to offer current, diverse information about important issues in our world, from a UK perspective.

ABOUT DISCUSSING SEXUAL HEALTH

Sexual health involves more than just being free from sexually transmitted infections (STIs) or not having to face unplanned pregnancy. It means taking responsibility for your body, and your partner's, as well as for your health and the decisions you make about sex. '15 things you should know about sex', 'Contraception myths' and soaring STI rates are just a few of the issues addressed in these pages. This book examines all aspects of sexual health; looking at the possible risks and dangers associated with sex and debating the issue of sex education.

OUR SOURCES

Titles in the *ISSUES* series are designed to function as educational resource books, providing a balanced overview of a specific subject.

The information in our books is comprised of facts, articles and opinions from many different sources, including:

- Newspaper reports and opinion pieces
- Website fact sheets
- Magazine and journal articles
- Statistics and surveys
- Government reports
- Literature from special interest groups

A NOTE ON CRITICAL EVALUATION

Because the information reprinted here is from a number of different sources, readers should bear in mind the origin of the text and whether the source is likely to have a particular bias when presenting information (or when conducting their research). It is hoped that, as you read about the many aspects of the issues explored in this book, you will critically evaluate the information presented.

It is important that you decide whether you are being presented with facts or opinions. Does the writer give a biased or unbiased report? If an opinion is being expressed, do you agree with the writer? Is there potential bias to the 'facts' or statistics behind an article?

ASSIGNMENTS

In the back of this book, you will find a selection of assignments designed to help you engage with the articles you have been reading and to explore your own opinions. Some tasks will take longer than others and there is a mixture of design, writing and research based activities that you can complete alone or in a group.

FURTHER RESEARCH

At the end of each article we have listed its source and a website that you can visit if you would like to conduct your own research. Please remember to critically evaluate any sources that you consult and consider whether the information you are viewing is accurate and unbiased.

D

Health

Independence Educational Publishers

First published by Independence Educational Publishers

The Studio, High Green

Great Shelford

Cambridge CB22 5EG

England

© Independence 2013

Copyright

Photocopy licence

British Library Cataloguing in Publication Data

Discussing sexual health. -- (Issues ; v. 237)

1. Sexually transmitted diseases. 2. Sexually transmitted diseases--Social aspects. 3. Hygiene, Sexual.

I. Series II. Acred, Cara.

616.9'51-dc23

ISBN-13: 9781 86168 635 0

Printed in Great Britain

MWL Print Group Ltd

What is sexual health?

Taking care of your sexual health means more than being free from sexually transmissible infections (STIs) or not having to face an unplanned pregnancy. It means taking responsibility for your body, your health, your partner's health and your decisions about sex.

Your body's changing

When you become a teenager, your body changes and develops towards sexual maturity (basically, you go from being a child to an adult). This is called 'puberty'. There are visible changes to your body as well as changes inside. Girls start having periods every month and their breasts grow. For guys, erections become much more frequent and unused sperm is released in semen during a 'wet dream' (usually at night during sleep). Being aware about these changes to your body and knowing they are a normal part of puberty is important.

Being safe with sex

Being safe with sex means caring for both your own health, and the health of your partner. This means being able to talk freely with your partner, both being ready for sex and agreeing on the use of condoms and a suitable type of contraception. Being safe protects you from getting or passing on sexually transmissible infections (STIs) and an unplanned pregnancy. You will enjoy good sexual health if you take care of your genitals (parts of your body that are involved in sex) and avoid any risky behaviour.

Talking about issues related to sex is also important for your mental health and well being. You should feel comfortable talking to your partner and medical professional about anything you are concerned about. Good mental health helps you to enjoy life, enjoy your relationships and enjoy sex.

What is safe sex?

We've all heard the term 'safe sex', but what exactly does it mean?

Being safe with sex means caring for both your own health, and the health of your partner. Being safe protects you from getting or passing on sexually transmissible infections (STIs) and an unplanned pregnancy. Whether you have vaginal, anal or oral sex, it definitely pays to play it safe!

And remember: There's more to sex than sexual intercourse!

There are lots of ways to enjoy physical intimacy with your partner without having oral, vaginal or anal sex. Safe sex also includes lots of other activities like kissing, cuddling, rubbing, massage, stroking, masturbation (touching your own genitals) or touching each other's genitals. Why not explore other ways to be intimate which do not put you at risk of sexually transmissible infections or an unintended pregnancy?

How you can stay safe?

Always use condoms if you have vaginal, oral or anal sex.

Use of condoms is the only method of contraception that protects against both STIs and pregnancy. Even if you're using other methods of contraception (like the pill or a diaphragm), always use condoms as well.

If you are having unprotected sex, talk to your partner about the risks involved. Remember your decision about safe sex is important, as some STIs can be cured but some can't, including HIV (Human Immunodeficiency Virus).

Before having sex, you need to discuss the use of condoms with your partner and come to an agreement about using condoms. Remember, you have the right to say NO if your partner does not agree to use condoms.

Never have sex (even with a condom) if your partner has a visible sore, ulcer or lump on their genitals or anal area. Suggest they see their doctor, family planning clinic or sexual health clinic.

STIs can be passed from one person to another by oral sex. If you put your month in contact with your partner's penis, you need to use a condom to avoid STIs. If you put your mouth in contact with your partner's anus or vulva (outside of vagina) while having sex, you need to use a dental dam (whether you are a guy or girl). This is especially important if you've got a cut or sore around your mouth or lips or bleeding gums.

STIs can also be transmitted if you use sex toys, so you need to be safe. Use condoms and change the condom for each person. Wash the toys carefully after use and wash your hands after removing the condom.

Don't be afraid to talk to your partner about sex.

Contraception

Contraception is a way to prevent pregnancy, and is sometimes called 'birth control'. Some forms of contraception such as condoms can also help reduce the spread of sexually transmissible infections (STIs). Contraception is a very important part of making sure sex is safe and being responsible for your actions.

There are several methods of contraception, including:

⇨ the pill – a tablet taken each day by girls to prevent pregnancy

⇨ condoms – a rubber sleeve worn on the penis

⇨ diaphragms – a rubber device worn inside the vagina

⇨ contraceptive implant (e.g. Implanon) – a device inserted under the skin of girls by a doctor which releases hormones to prevent pregnancy.

'Condoms can also help reduce the spread of sexually transmissible infections'

There is also a form of contraception called the emergency contraception pill, which can help prevent unintended pregnancy. It can be taken by girls within 72 hours after unprotected sex, although preferably within 24 hours. It is available across the counter at chemists or from your local GP, family planning clinic or sexual health clinic.

It's important to talk about contraception with your partner and decide how you will handle any issues before having sex. You both have to be happy with the choice

and make sure you're aware of any risks involved.

Condoms

A condom is a rubber sleeve worn by guys on their penis. Using a condom is very important to help protect you from STIs, including HIV. But remember, some STIs such as genital herpes and genital warts can spread from person to person even when condoms are used.

Tips for using condoms

⇨ Buying correctly. Condoms are available in chemist shops, supermarkets, some petrol stations, and through vending machines. Get the ones that fit you.

⇨ Buying incorrectly. Gimmick shops often sell 'party' condoms. Make sure you only use Australian standard quality approved condoms!

⇨ Storing correctly. Store condoms in a cool, dark place. Only carry them temporarily in your wallet or handbag.

⇨ Storing incorrectly. Keep condoms away from heat (e.g. sunlight) and sharp objects (e.g. ear stud).

⇨ Opening correctly. Tear packet open gently.

⇨ Opening incorrectly. Do not open packet with your teeth, sharp fingernails or scissors.

⇨ Correct lubricants. Always use water-based lubricant.

⇨ Incorrect lubricants. Never use oil-based lubricants.

⇨ Correct condom disposal. Tie the condom in a knot and put it in the bin.

⇨ Incorrect condom disposal. Flushing condoms down the toilet harms the environment.

Other things to remember

⇨ Check the expiry date. Don't use condoms that have expired. Before use, check the condom has not discoloured or become brittle.

⇨ Find the type of condom that suits you and fits well. A condom that's too tight can break and a condom that's too loose can fall off.

⇨ Never use a condom that you have tried to put on inside out as it may have been contaminated. Always use a new condom. Never re-use a condom.

⇨ Some people find certain brands of condoms irritate their skin. Try other brands.

⇨ As fluid may leak out as soon as the penis is hard, put the condom on before the penis goes near your partner's genitals, mouth or anus.

'Don't be afraid to talk to your partner about sex'

What to do if the condom breaks

Stay calm, and withdraw the penis immediately.

Wash the genitals with water (not soap or detergent) and pass urine. Girls shouldn't douche or spray water into their vagina – this can increase the risk of catching a STI.

Once you've removed the condom, be careful not to allow the condom or the penis to touch your partner's genitals, mouth or anus.

Wash your hands after removing the condom.

If there is a risk of pregnancy or exposure to an STI, talk to your local doctor, family planning clinic or sexual health clinic. It's always worth having a check-up.

⇨ The above information is reprinted with kind permission from The State of Queensland. Please visit www.health.qld. gov.au for more information on this and other subjects.

© The State of Queensland (Queensland Health) 2010

15 things you should know about sex

Information from NHS Choices.

1: You can get pregnant the first time that you have sex.

You may have heard that a girl can't get pregnant the first time that she has sex. The truth is, if a boy and a girl have sex and don't use contraception, she can get pregnant, whether it's her first time or she has had sex lots of times.

A boy can get a girl pregnant the first time he has sex. If you're female and have sex, you can get pregnant as soon as you start ovulating (releasing eggs). This happens before you have your first period. Find out more about periods and the menstrual cycle.

Using contraception protects against pregnancy. Using condoms also protects against sexually transmitted infections (STIs). Before you have sex, talk to your partner about contraception, and make sure you've got some contraception. Find out about getting contraception and tips on using condoms.

2: You can get pregnant if a boy withdraws (pulls out) his penis before he comes.

There's a myth that a girl can't get pregnant if a boy withdraws his penis before he ejaculates (comes). The truth is, pulling out the penis won't stop a girl from getting pregnant.

Before a boy ejaculates, there's sperm in the pre-ejaculatory fluid (pre-come), which leaks out when he gets excited. It only takes one sperm to get a girl pregnant. Pre-come can contain sexually transmitted infections (STIs), so withdrawing the penis won't prevent you from getting an infection.

If a boy says he'll take care to withdraw before he ejaculates, don't believe him. Nobody can stop themselves from leaking sperm before they come. Always use a condom to protect yourself against STIs, and also use other contraception to prevent unwanted pregnancy.

3: You can get pregnant if you have sex during your period.

There's a myth that a girl can't get pregnant if she has sex during her period. The truth is, she can get pregnant at any time of the month if she has sex without contraception.

Sperm can survive for several days after sex, so even if you do it during your period, sperm can stay in the body long enough to get you pregnant.

4: You can get pregnant if you have sex standing up, sitting down or in any other position.

You may have heard the myth that a girl can't get pregnant if she has sex standing up, sitting down, or if she jumps up and down afterwards. The truth is, there's no such thing as a 'safe' position if you're having sex without a condom or another form of contraception.

There are also no 'safe' places to have sex, including the bath or shower. Pregnancy can happen whatever position you do it in, and wherever you do it. All that's needed is for a sperm to meet an egg.

5: You can't get pregnant by having oral sex.

You may have heard that you can get pregnant by having oral sex. The truth is, a girl can't get pregnant this way, even if she swallows sperm. But you can catch STIs through oral sex, including gonorrhoea, chlamydia and herpes. It's safer to use a condom on a penis, and a dam (a very thin, soft plastic square that acts as a barrier) over the female genitals if you have oral sex.

6: Drinking alcohol doesn't make you better in bed.

There's a myth that drinking alcohol makes you perform better in bed. The truth is, when you're drunk it's hard to make smart decisions. Alcohol can make you take risks, such as having sex before you're ready, or having sex with someone you don't like. Drinking won't make the experience better. You're more likely to regret having sex if you do it when you're drunk. Find out more about sex and alcohol.

7: You can't use clingfilm, plastic bags, crisp packets or anything else instead of a condom. They won't work

There's a myth that you can use a plastic bag, clingfilm or a crisp packet instead of a condom. The truth is, you can't. Only a condom can protect against STIs.

You can get condoms free from:

⇨ community contraceptive clinics

⇨ sexual health and genitourinary medicine (GUM) clinics

⇨ some young persons services

You can also buy them from pharmacies and shops. Make sure that they have the CE mark on them, as this means that they've been tested to European safety standards. Find sexual health services near you, including contraception clinics.

8: A boy's testicles (balls) will not explode if he doesn't have sex.

You may have heard the myth that if a boy doesn't have sex his balls will explode. The truth is, not having sex doesn't harm boys or girls, and a boy's balls will not explode.

Boys and men produce sperm all the time. If they don't ejaculate the sperm is absorbed into their body. Ejaculation can happen if they masturbate or have a wet dream. They don't have to have sex. Find out about boys' bodies.

9: Condoms can't be washed out and used again.

Don't believe anyone who says that you can wash condoms and use them again. The truth is, you can't use a condom more than once, even if you wash it out. If you've used a condom, throw it away and use a new one if you have sex again.

This is true for male condoms and female condoms. Condoms need to be changed after 30 minutes of sex because friction can weaken the condom, making it more likely to break or fail. Get tips on using condoms.

10: You can get pregnant if you have sex only once.

You may have heard the myth that you have to have sex lots of times to get pregnant. The truth is, you can get pregnant if you have sex once. All it takes is for one sperm to meet an egg. To avoid pregnancy, always use contraception, and use a condom to protect against STIs.

11: You don't always get symptoms if you have an STI.

You may have heard the myth that you'd always know if you had an STI because it would hurt when you pee, or you'd notice a discharge, unusual smell or soreness. This isn't true.

Many people don't notice signs of infection, so you won't always know if you're infected. You can't tell by looking at someone whether they've got an STI. If you're worried that you've caught an STI, visit your GP or local sexual health clinic. Check-ups and tests for STIs are free and confidential, including for under-16s. Find out about sexual health services near you.

12: Women who have sex with women can get STIs.

You may have heard that women who sleep with women can't get or pass on STIs. This isn't true. If a woman has an STI and has sex with another woman, the infection can be passed on through vaginal fluid (including fluid on shared sex toys), blood or close body contact.

Always use condoms on shared sex toys, and use dams to cover the genitals during oral sex. A dam is a very thin, soft plastic square that acts as a barrier to prevent infection (ask about dams at a pharmacist or sexual health clinic). If a woman is also having sex with a man, using contraception and condoms will help to prevent STIs and unintended pregnancy.

13: Not all gay men have anal sex.

You may have heard that all gay men have anal sex. This isn't true. Anal sex, like any sexual activity, is a matter of preference. Some people choose to do it as part of their sex life and some don't, whether they're gay, straight, lesbian or bisexual.

According to the National Survey of Sexual Attitudes and Lifestyles (taken in 2000), 12.3% of men and 11.3% of women had had anal sex in the previous year. Whatever sex you have, use a condom to protect yourself and your partner against STIs. However, having sex isn't the only way to show your feelings for someone.

14: A girl is not ready to have sex just because she's started her periods.

You may have heard that a girl should be having sex once she starts having periods. This isn't true. Starting your periods means that you're growing up, and that you could get pregnant if you were to have sex. It doesn't mean that you're ready to have sex, or that you should be sexually active. People feel ready to have sex at different times. It's a personal decision. Most young people in England wait until they're 16 or older before they start having sex. Find out more about periods and the menstrual cycle.

15: Help is available if you need it.

If you want to talk to someone in confidence, you can call the Sexual Health Helpline on 0800 567 123.

30 September 2011

⇨ The above information is reprinted with kind permission from NHS Choices. Please visit www. nhs.uk for further information.

Sexual health quiz

From www.under-cover.org.uk

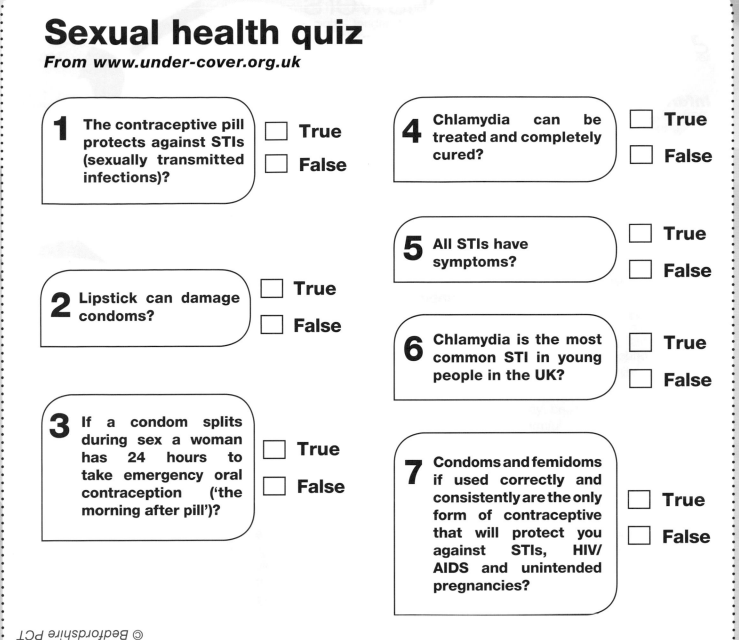

1 The contraceptive pill protects against STIs (sexually transmitted infections)?
☐ True
☐ False

2 Lipstick can damage condoms?
☐ True
☐ False

3 If a condom splits during sex a woman has 24 hours to take emergency oral contraception ('the morning after pill')?
☐ True
☐ False

4 Chlamydia can be treated and completely cured?
☐ True
☐ False

5 All STIs have symptoms?
☐ True
☐ False

6 Chlamydia is the most common STI in young people in the UK?
☐ True
☐ False

7 Condoms and femidoms if used correctly and consistently are the only form of contraceptive that will protect you against STIs, HIV/AIDS and unintended pregnancies?
☐ True
☐ False

© *Bedfordshire PCT*

⇨ The above information is reprinted with kind permission from Bedfordshire PCT. Please visit www.under-cover.org.uk for further information.

Answers

1. FALSE – Contraceptive pills do not protect against STIs or HIV/AIDS. They do protect against pregnancy if used correctly.

2. TRUE – Any contact with oil-based products can damage condoms. These include:

– Massage Oils
– Baby Oil
– Sun Tan Creams and Oils
– Cooking Oil
– Ice Cream
– Mayonnaise
– Petroleum Jelly (Vaseline)
– Moisturiser

Water based lubricants are safe to use with condoms.

3. FALSE – The emergency contraceptive pill can be taken within 72 hours. However the sooner it is taken the more effective it is.

4. TRUE – If you test positive for Chlamydia, you will be offered free antibiotics.

5. FALSE – Not all STIs will have symptoms. For example Chlamydia often has no signs or symptoms.

6. TRUE – Chlamydia is the UK's most common curable sexually transmitted infection. It is caused by bacteria and is easily passed on through unprotected anal, oral or vaginal sex or by fingers with an infected person. Chlamydia often has no signs or symptoms.

7. TRUE – Other forms of contraception such as the coil, cap, pill, implant and injection may give some protection against pregnancy but will not protect against sexually transmitted infections.

'Clueless or clued up: your right to be informed about contraception' media report

World Contraception Day 2011.

The 'clueless or clued up: your right to be informed about contraception' media report explores young people's attitudes to sex and contraception, and specifically whether they are able to access accurate and unbiased information about contraception and make informed decisions about their sexual and reproductive health.

The report, written and sponsored by Bayer Healthcare Pharmaceuticals, includes the perspectives of 5,426 young people across 26 countries in Asia Pacific, Europe, Latin America and the USA. 600 young people were also surveyed in Egypt, Kenya and Uganda.

What do the findings tell us?

Young people are still having unprotected sex with new partners for a variety of reasons and knowledge of effective and reliable contraceptive methods is less than optimal. In some countries included in the survey, the situation appears to be getting worse year on year.

In terms of information access, young people appear to be gathering insights about sex and contraception from a wide variety of sources including magazines, the Internet, friends and family as well as from healthcare professionals and school. With the Internet being the overall preferred source of information about sex and contraception, it is also cited as the second most common source of inaccurate information and clearly much of what young people read in social media sites or forums could well be myth or misconception. This is highlighted by the large numbers of young people who believe that ineffective methods of contraception, such as the 'withdrawal method' or having sex during menstruation, will protect them from an unplanned pregnancy.

A considerable number of young people said they have received information on contraception that they have since realised was inaccurate or untrue – in most cases the information was obtained from friends or the Internet but in some cases it was provided by partners or even teachers.

The fact that school does not provide a comfortable environment for questions about sexuality and intimacy was raised as a common barrier preventing young people from being able to obtain accurate and unbiased information on contraception.

In addition to this, the survey results appear to suggest that in some countries there may be a link between poor provision of sex education at school and numbers of unplanned pregnancies, for example in Brazil and Indonesia where there is limited sex education, as many as 67% and 48% of young people have a close friend or family member who has had an unplanned pregnancy. Furthermore, in France and Norway, where 85% and 84% of young people receive sex education, only 25% and 24%, know a close friend or family member who has had an unplanned pregnancy. There is also some correlation between poor provision of sex education and prevalence of misconceptions about effective contraceptive methods – in Turkey and Russia where education provision is low, a large number of young people believe that unreliable methods such as withdrawal or bathing/showering after sex are effective at preventing an unplanned pregnancy.

However, there are exceptions to this, such as in Poland, where 69% of teenagers receive sex education but as many as 56% know someone who has had an unplanned pregnancy. This could suggest that in some countries where there is widespread provision of sex education, the quality of it, in terms of how young people are taught and the topics covered, may vary from school to school and from region to region. Poor services and supplies are also likely to be a factor in the levels of unplanned pregnancies and poor contraception knowledge in some countries, although the survey does not investigate these issues extensively.

No matter where they live, respondents told us that they are too embarrassed to ask for information and that they were unable to access contraception when they needed it because they were too embarrassed to ask a healthcare professional – the very person charged with supplying them with accurate and unbiased information and family planning supplies.

All young people have the right to learn about their sexual and reproductive health and about the importance of asserting one's sexual health rights so they are able to make empowered and informed choices. World Contraception Day 2011, under the theme of 'Live Your Life, Know Your Rights, Learn About Contraception' focuses on the right of young people to access accurate and unbiased information about contraception in order to prevent an unplanned pregnancy or sexually transmitted infection (STI).

Although these survey results report on the incidence of unprotected sex, it is important to note that contraception should always be used to prevent an unplanned pregnancy and/or STI when having sex with a new partner and during a stable relationship.

Did you know...

Young people today

⇨ Nearly half of the world's population (almost three billion people) is under the age of 25[1]

⇨ 44% of young people prioritise personal hygiene, including showering, waxing and applying perfume, above contraception when preparing for a date that may lead to sex[2]

⇨ Studies show that young people do not consider the Internet as the most trustworthy source of information about contraception[3]

1   World Population Foundation website (Last accessed July 2011)
    http://www.wpf.org/reproductive_rights_article/facts

2   Bayer HealthCare Pharmaceuticals. Data on file. Contraception: Whose responsibility is it anyway? Survey. Fieldwork carried out by GFK Healthcare. May 2010

3   Jones, R., et al, Teens Reflect on Their Sources of Contraceptive Information, Guttmacher Institute 2007

⇨ A young person's mother is the second most trusted source of information about sex and contraception after a doctor. Although, young people feel most comfortable approaching their partner for information[4]

⇨ Embarrassment is a key risk factor in young people's sexual behaviour, this can mean that they resist seeking information and advice about sex and contraception[5]

⇨ School-based sex education delays rather than hastens the onset of sexual activity[6]

⇨ Across the world, inhabitants of 213 countries currently use Facebook[7] – in the countries involved in the WCD 2011 multi-national survey more than 100,000,000 young people (15-19-year-olds) are registered users of the social networking site[8]

4   Bayer HealthCare Pharmaceuticals. Data on file. Talking Sex and Contraception Survey. Fieldwork carried out by TNS Healthcare. July 2009

5   Bell, J. Why embarrassment inhibits the acquisition and use of condoms: A qualitative approach to understanding risky sexual behaviour, J Adolesc. 2009 Apr; 32(2):379-91. Epub 2008 Aug 8

6   Wellings, K., et al, Sexual behaviour in context: a global perspective. The Lancet Sexual and Reproductive Health Series, October 2006

7   Social Bakers online (Last accessed: August 2011)
    http://www.socialbakers.com/facebook-statistics/

8   Facebook advertising information accessible online (Last accessed: August 2011) http://www.facebook.com/ads/create/

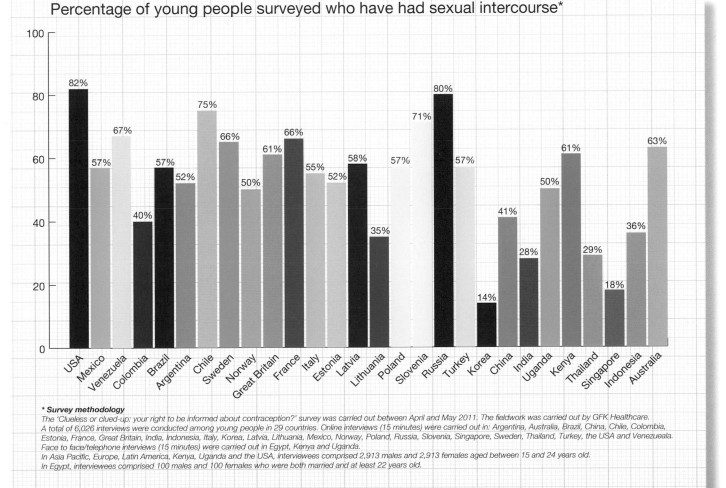

Percentage of young people surveyed who have had sexual intercourse*

USA 82%, Mexico 57%, Venezuela 67%, Colombia 40%, Brazil 57%, Argentina 52%, Chile 75%, Sweden 66%, Norway 50%, Great Britain 61%, France 66%, Italy 55%, Estonia 52%, Latvia 58%, Lithuania 35%, Poland 57%, Slovenia 71%, Russia 80%, Turkey 57%, Korea 14%, China 41%, India 28%, Uganda 50%, Kenya 61%, Thailand 29%, Singapore 18%, Indonesia 36%, Australia 63%

* Survey methodology
The 'Clueless or clued-up: your right to be informed about contraception?' survey was carried out between April and May 2011. The fieldwork was carried out by GFK Healthcare.
A total of 6,026 interviews were conducted among young people in 29 countries. Online interviews (15 minutes) were carried out in: Argentina, Australia, Brazil, China, Chile, Colombia, Estonia, France, Great Britain, India, Indonesia, Italy, Korea, Latvia, Lithuania, Mexico, Norway, Poland, Russia, Slovenia, Singapore, Sweden, Thailand, Turkey, the USA and Venezuela.
Face to face/telephone interviews (15 minutes) were carried out in Egypt, Kenya and Uganda.
In Asia Pacific, Europe, Latin America, Kenya, Uganda and the USA, interviewees comprised 2,913 males and 2,913 females aged between 15 and 24 years old.
In Egypt, interviewees comprised 100 males and 100 females who were both married and at least 22 years old.

Source: 'Clueless or clued up: your right to be informed about contraception' media report, 2011, Bayer Health Care Pharmaceuticals © Bayer HealthCare Pharmaceuticals

Incidence of unplanned pregnancies and sexually transmitted infections

⇨ Worldwide, more than 41% of the 208 million pregnancies that occur each year are unintended[9]

⇨ Every year, 14-16 million adolescent females aged 15 to 19 give birth, and pregnancy-related deaths are the leading cause of death for young women this age[10]

⇨ If unmet need for contraception was fully satisfied, each year 53 million more unintended pregnancies could be prevented[11]

⇨ 15% of young adults between the ages of 18 and 26 have had a sexually transmitted disease in the past year[12]

⇨ Ten million women die as a result of pregnancy-related conditions each generation[13]

⇨ One in 20 adolescent girls get a bacterial infection through sexual contact every year and the age at which infections are acquired is becoming younger and younger[14]

⇨ Young adults (15-24 years old) make up only 25% of the sexually active population, but represent almost 50% of all new acquired sexually transmitted diseases[15]

⇨ In 2007, teenagers in the United States were eight times more likely to give birth than teenagers in the Netherlands[16]

⇨ In 2009 there were 38.3 conceptions per thousand women aged 15-17 in England and Wales[17]

Impact of unplanned pregnancies and sexually transmitted infections

⇨ Every £1 invested in contraception saves the UK National Health Service £11 plus additional welfare costs, which is a powerful economic argument for maintaining contraceptive services[18]

⇨ The 1990s witnessed significant gains in access to reproductive health and family planning, but in many less developed countries (LDCs), particularly from Africa, the progress has come to a stand-still since about 2000[19]

⇨ Unplanned pregnancies constitute a global problem associated with substantial costs to health and social services and emotional distress to women, their families and society as a whole[20]

⇨ Having a child early in life may lead to a number of potential disadvantages for both mother and child. Particularly for young teenagers, pregnancy not only carries considerable risks for their health and that of their offspring, but it is also a factor of social, cultural and economic failure[21]

⇨ Children born to teenage mothers are much more likely to experience a range of negative outcomes in later life, such as developmental disabilities, behavioural issues and poor academic performance[22]

⇨ Teen childbearing in the United States costs taxpayers (federal, state and local) at least $9.1 billion annually[23]

⇨ Unintended pregnancy is a key contributor to the rapid population growth that in turn impairs social welfare, hinders economic progress, and exacerbates environmental degradation[24]

⇨ Overall, the cost – just to the National Health Service (NHS) – of teenage pregnancy is estimated to be £69 million annually[25]

⇨ The above information is reprinted with kind permission from Bayer HealthCare Pharmaceuticals. Please visit www.your-life.com for further information.

9 Singh, S., et al. Unintended pregnancy: worldwide levels, trends, and outcomes. Stud Fam Plann (2010)41(4): 241-250

10 Blake, S. et al., Youth Guide for Action on Maternal Health, Women Deliver 2010

11 Global Maternal Mortality Fact Sheet http://www.mothersdayeveryday.org/docs/MDED_FactSheet.pdf

12 Wildsmith, E., et al., Sexually Transmitted Diseases among Young Adults: Prevalence, Perceived Risk, and Risk-Taking Behaviours, Child Trends Research Brief 2010

13 Women deliver website (last accessed May 2011) http://www.womendeliver.org/about/the-issue/

14 WHO 10 facts on sexually transmitted infections, WHO Fact File (Last accessed: August 2011) http://www.who.int/features/factfiles/sexually_transmitted_diseases/facts/en/index2.html

15 Ros et al., Global epidemiology of sexually transmitted diseases. Asian J Androl. 2008 Jan;10(1):110-4.

16 John S. et al., A New Vision for Adolescent Sexual and Reproductive Health, ACT for Youth Center of Excellence

17 Office for National Statistics. Statistical Bulletin. Conceptions in England and Wales 2009.

18 TEENAGE PREGNANCY INDEPENDENT ADVISORY GROUP FINAL REPORT, Teenage pregnancy: Past successes – future challenges

19 Population Dynamics in the Least Developed Countries: Challenges and Opportunities for Development and Poverty Reduction, United Nations population fund, 2011

20 Mavranezouli I et al. Health economics of contraception. Best Practice & Research Clinical Obstetrics and Gynaecology 2009;23:187-198

21 Amy JJ et al. Pregnancy during adolescence: A major social problem. The European Journal of Contraception & Reproductive Health Care. 2007; 12(4): 299-302

22 Hofferth S L et al. Early childbearing and Children's Achievement and Behaviour Over Time. Perspectives on Sexual and Reproductive Health. 2002; 34(1): 41-49

23 NATIONAL CAMPAIGN TO PREVENT TEEN PREGNANCY, By the Numbers: The Public Costs of Teen Childbearing in Texas, http://www.thenationalcampaign.org/costs/pdf/states/texas/fact-sheet.pdf November 2006

24 Speidel, J. et al. Addressing Global Health, Economic, and Environmental Problems Through Family Planning Obstetrics & Gynecology: June 2011 - Volume 117 - Issue 6 - pp 1394-1398

25 Teenage Pregnancy Independent Advisory Group, Annual report 2008 from Teenage Pregnancy Independent Advisory Group http://publicpolicyexchange.co.uk/docs/8J02-PPE_4_Gill_Frances.pdf

Contraception myths

By Kaveh Manavi, for Whittall Street Clinic.

MYTH! 'I don't need contraception because I only have sex during the 'safe' time'

Ovulation (release of egg cell in women) is the result of a delicate balance between four different hormones. Identification of the exact time of ovulation is not easy and requires careful monitoring of several menstrual cycles before using this method. Because of its complexity, this is not a reliable method of contraception. **FACT**

MYTH! 'A woman can't get pregnant if she doesn't have an orgasm'

While the man must ejaculate to release sperm, it is not necessary for the woman to have an orgasm to get pregnant. Ovulation (release of egg) in women can occur without having sex or an orgasm. **FACT**

MYTH! 'I won't get pregnant if we have sex standing up or if I am on top'

The sperm by nature move up through the cervical canal after ejaculation. The woman's position during sex has no effect on the sperm's movement into the womb. Similarly, jumping up and down after sex cannot prevent pregnancy.

MYTH! 'I won't get pregnant if my partner pulls out before he ejaculates'

Pulling out before the man ejaculates is not a reliable method of contraception. Some fluid that contains sperm might be released before the man actually begins to climax. Also, some men might not have the willpower or be able to withdraw in time. **FACT**

MYTH! 'You will not become pregnant if you take a shower or bath right after sex, or if you urinate right after sex'

Washing or urinating after sex will not stop sperm that have already entered through the cervix. **FACT**

MYTH! '"The pill" is effective immediately after you begin taking it'

In most women, one complete menstrual cycle is needed for the hormones in the pill (oral contraceptive) to prevent ovulation. **FACT**

MYTH! 'You can use plastic wrap if you don't have a condom'

Plastic wrap cannot be used as condoms. Condoms are specifically made to provide a good fit and good protection during sex, and they are thoroughly tested for maximum effectiveness. **FACT**

MYTH! 'Toothpaste kills the sperm'

Toothpastes have no effect on the sperm and cannot replace spermicides. **FACT**

MYTH! 'A woman cannot become pregnant if she has sex during her period'

It is true that a woman having her period is not ovulating. The time of ovulation in women may be irregular however. Because sperm can live inside a women's body for five days, a woman who ovulates within seven days of having sex can get pregnant. Having unprotected sex during your period is not a reliable method of contraception. **FACT**

⇨ The above information is reprinted with kind permission from Whittall Street Clinic. Please visit www.whittallstreet.nhs.uk.

Sexual consent and the law

Information from This is Abuse.

The law

Rape is when a man forces his penis into the vagina, anus or mouth of another person when that person doesn't want him to do so; the law calls this 'without consent'.

The most important bit to remember is that being pressured or forced to have sex when you don't want to is a crime.

Sexual assault is a crime that can be committed by both men and women against men or women. Different types of sexual assault include:

⇨ Objects or parts of the body (e.g. a finger) being put into someone's vagina or anus when that person didn't want it to happen.

⇨ Someone being touched in a sexual way that makes him or her feel uncomfortable or frightened. This could be through their clothes (like bottom pinching).

⇨ Someone being made to sexually stimulate themselves using their hands or fingers (known as masturbation).

⇨ Any other form of physical closeness that happens without consent is known as sexual assault. It can also include; watching other people: having sex, 'sexting' (texting sexual images), and forcing involvement in watching or making pornography.

Consent – what it means

Consent

Consent is someone giving permission or agreeing to something, after they have thought carefully about whether or not they want to do something.

To be able to give your consent you should be sure that it is your decision and not one you have been pressured to make.

The law in Britain says that both people need to give their consent before sex or any physical closeness.

The law also says that to consent to sex a person must be over 16 and have the ability to make informed decisions for themselves.

Being pressured

If you are being forced or pressured into doing sexual things you don't like or aren't sure about, then this is abuse. There are ways someone might try to make you do things without physically forcing you, these can include:

⇨ Being made to feel stupid or bad for saying 'no'.

⇨ Being bullied into having sex.

⇨ Being encouraged to drink lots of alcohol or take drugs to make you more likely to have sex.

⇨ Manipulating your emotions, for example saying 'If you loved me you would...'.

Making sure you have got consent

⇨ Sex with any girl/boy under 16 is unlawful, including oral. It doesn't make any difference if permission (consent) is given or not, if you're under 16 sex is illegal.

⇨ Consent to one sort of sexual activity does not mean you are getting consent to everything. Permission is required for each activity.

⇨ Consent may be withdrawn at any time. If your partner changes their mind, it's their right to do so.

⇨ Even if you have had sex with someone before, you still need permission the next time.

⇨ Giving oral sex to someone without permission is rape.

⇨ If you do not get consent – it's rape.

'Sex with any girl/boy under 16 is unlawful... it doesn't make any difference if permission (consent) is given or not'

More things to look out for to make sure you have consent

When it comes to sex or physical closeness you should feel safe with your partner, be able to trust them and feel that they would respect you whatever your decision.

Good communication between you both will help to ensure you know how your partner feels about sex or physical closeness. It is a good idea to check things out with your partner by asking if they are enjoying what you are doing and asking if they want to continue.

Reading body language is also important. If your partner is relaxed it is likely that they feel comfortable. If they are tense, they may be nervous or frightened and are probably trying to hide how they really feel.

Someone doesn't have to say the word 'NO' to withhold their permission, there are lots of ways they might say they don't want to do something or have sex.

Sometimes people might find it hard to say anything at all if they don't want to have sex, so you should always look out for other signs that they might not be comfortable and might not be giving their consent.

Consequences

What are 'consequences'?

Everything that a person does has an affect on something or someone. This effect is known as a 'consequence'. Consequences can either be positive or negative.

Both positive and negative consequences can have a lasting impact on people's lives.

Sex or physical closeness without consent can have negative consequences for both people involved.

What are the consequences if you have been pressured into sex?

Health

Potential health consequences could include: unwanted pregnancy, sexually transmitted infections for both you and your partner, physical damage, internal injury, mental health problems, depression and self-harm.

Emotional

Potential emotional consequences can include: lower self-esteem and sense of worth, humiliation, fear and hurt.

What are the consequences if you have done the pressuring?

Legal

Having sex without gaining consent could potentially lead to you spending up to eight years in prison.

Sexually assaulting another person could lead to a community order, fine or prison sentence

Both having sex without consent and sexual assault could lead to your details being put on the Sex Offenders' Register.

Health

Potential consequences could include sexually transmitted infections for both you and your partner.

Social

Potential consequences could include being labelled an abuser by people who know you.

What should I do?

Who should I tell if I have been raped or sexually assaulted?

Understand that this was not your fault. There was nothing you could have done to prevent the assault. Nothing you did gave anyone the right to do this. The fault lies entirely with the person who raped or sexually assaulted you.

Firstly, it is important you tell someone as soon as possible and not keep it to yourself. Telling someone what has happened means that you can get the support you need. The person you do talk to should be someone that you trust and feel comfortable with. You may choose to tell: a friend, parent, GP or a school teacher.

You can also speak to the police. Most police forces have specially trained police officers. You can contact the police immediately by dialling 999.

Whether they had had sex or not, respondents were asked whether they would find it easy to access contraception, if they needed any. 62 per cent said they would find this easy. Females and males did not differ significantly in their response to this question

Sexual experience

Around one quarter of respondents (26 per cent) reported that they had had sex. 46 per cent of these were 16 years of age when they did so, 31 per cent were 15 years old whilst the remaining 22 per cent were younger. Proportionately, females were slightly more likely than males to say that they had had sex (28 per cent and 23 per cent respectively). However, among respondents who had had sex, males were much more likely to say that they had done so before they were 16 years of age (61 per cent) than females (49 per cent). 12 per cent of males and two per cent of females who had had sex, said they had sex at least once with a same-sex partner.

Most respondents (81 per cent) who had had sex said they or their partners had used a condom when they first had sex. Nine per cent of all respondents who had had sex said they did not use any means of contraception when they first had sex or they could not remember whether they did.

YLT asked respondents to reflect on the timing of the first time they had sex: 30 per cent said that this had happened on the spur of the moment, whilst 29 per cent said they had planned this together with their partners. Males were much more likely than females to say that it just happened on the spur of the moment (40 per cent and 23 per cent respectively) whilst females were more likely than males to say that they had planned this together with their partner beforehand (31 per cent and 25 per cent respectively). Ten per cent of females but only one per cent of males said that they didn't really want to have sex but felt they should or that they were forced into having sex.

Looking back, 62 per cent of respondents felt that the first time they had sex came at the right time; however, 34 per cent felt it happened too early. Research shows that the older respondents were when they first had sex, the more likely they were to say that the timing was right. Seven out of ten respondents who had sex before they were 14 years of age felt that this was too early. In contrast, nearly three quarters (73 per cent) of those who first had sex at 16 years of age felt that this was the right time.

Respondents were asked for the reasons why they first had sex. Multiple responses were possible in this question. The table below shows that curiosity and the feeling that sex seemed like a natural follow-on to the relationship were the two main reasons why both males and females said they first had sex. The

third most common reason overall given by respondents for having sex was that they were in love, however, females were much more likely to say this (43 per cent) than males (29 per cent). In fact, males were more likely to say that they wanted to lose their virginity (32 per cent) than that they were to say that they were in love (29 per cent). Females and males were equally likely to say that they had sex because everyone else seemed to be doing it (28 per cent and 29 per cent respectively). The graph also shows that more females than males felt not ready to have sex and that only females said they were forced to have sex against their wishes.

Respondents were asked how long the relationship with their first sexual partner continued and how many sexual partners they have had. The lower pie chart on page 17 shows that about one third (31 per cent) of the respondents who had had sex said that they were still in the relationship with this first partner. On the other hand, one in five respondents said that their relationship had not continued at all after they had sex. Females (35 per cent) were much more likely to say that their relationship was still continuing than males (24 per cent). In contrast, males (24 per cent) were more likely than females (17 per cent) to say that their relationship had not continued at all. The earlier respondents said they had sex, the more likely they were to say that the relationship did not continue at all.

As the upper pie chart on page 17 shows, over half of respondents (54 per cent) said they had had one sexual partner only. Only eight per cent of respondents said that they had more than five sexual partners. Females and males did not differ significantly in respect to the number of sexual partners they had.

Just over one in four respondents (26 per cent) who had had sex had used after-sex contraception (or 'emergency contraception'). 16 per cent had used this once, eight per cent two or three times, and two per cent more than three times.

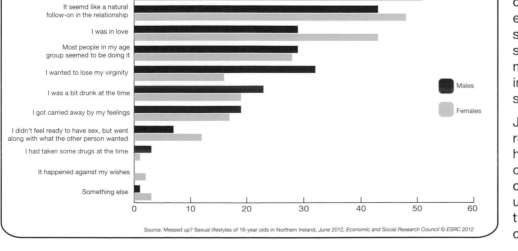

Which of the following things applied to you at the time you first had sex? By gender (%)

- I was curious about what it would be like
- It seemd like a natural follow-on in the relationship
- I was in love
- Most people in my age group seemed to be doing it
- I wanted to lose my virginity
- I was a bit drunk at the time
- I got carried away by my feelings
- I didn't feel ready to have sex, but went along with what the other person wanted
- I had taken some drugs at the time
- It happened against my wishes
- Something else

■ Males
▨ Females

Source: Messed up? Sexual lifestyles of 16-year olds in Northern Ireland, June 2012, Economic and Social Research Council © ESRC 2012

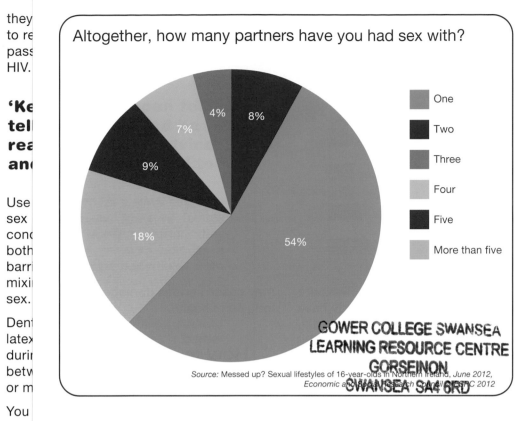

Altogether, how many partners have you had sex with?

- One
- Two
- Three
- Four
- Five
- More than five

8%
4%
7%
9%
18%
54%

Source: Messed up? Sexual lifestyles of 16-year-olds in Northern Ireland, *June 2012, Economic and Social Research Council © ESRC 2012*

they
to re
pass
HIV.

**'Ke
tel
rea
an**

Use
sex
cond
both
barr
mixi
sex.

Dent
late
durir
betw
or m

You
all ki

⇨ I
⇨ C
⇨ F
    (
    S
⇨ C

Or b

⇨ C
⇨ F
⇨ N
    a

**'Ev
usi
of (
pre
the
use**

Si

Man
Som
dont
or tr
to s(

Keep
and

Conclusions

The results of the 2011 YLT survey show that nearly three quarters of 16-year-olds had not had sex. Among those who did, almost half said having sex for them was a natural follow-on in the relationship they were in at the time. About one in three had planned their first sexual encounter together with their partner, and three in ten were still in a relationship with their first sexual partner. Looking back, six in ten respondents said that their first sex came at the right time for them. The majority of those who had had sex only had one sexual partner. Eight in ten respondents used a barrier method (condom) when they first had sex which protects them from sexual transmitted infections.

All these findings are myth-busters in the face of those who portray young people as irresponsible, promiscuous, sexed-up beings who don't think much about the consequences of entering a sexual relationship. However, the findings also show that those teaching sexuality education with a 'no sex before marriage' agenda need to acknowledge that many young people don't make this choice. The YLT data clearly show that school-based sex education is young people's preferred choice as they find this most trustworthy. However, in order not to fail young people, the YLT findings suggest that a more open and positive approach is required for this.

Apart from the standard of sex education, there are some other reasons for concern. The findings clearly show that the later respondents have sex the less they are likely to regret this and the more they are likely to be in a stable relationship with their partner. One third of males also said they had sex because they wanted to lose their virginity, which would be an indication that especially young males may still experience pressure from their peer group to have sex. As one respondent commented:

'I know a number of 12-14-year olds who are already considering to have sex simply because their friends have said they had.'

So, is the sexual health of 16-year-olds in Northern Ireland just 'messed up' as one 16-year-old felt? Whilst there is little reason to be as negative as some of the respondents were themselves, there is no room for complacency and still much more work to be done so that young people feel they can openly discuss sexual matters with adults.

June 2012

⇨ The above information is reprinted with kind permission from ARK. Please visit www.ark. ac.uk for further information.

© 2012 ARK

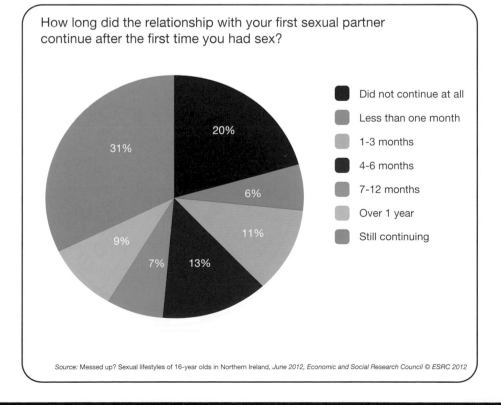

How long did the relationship with your first sexual partner continue after the first time you had sex?

- Did not continue at all
- Less than one month
- 1-3 months
- 4-6 months
- 7-12 months
- Over 1 year
- Still continuing

20%
31%
6%
11%
9%
7%
13%

Source: Messed up? Sexual lifestyles of 16-year olds in Northern Ireland, *June 2012, Economic and Social Research Council © ESRC 2012*

Types of STIs

Details about some of the most common STIs.

Chlamydia

The most common STI in the UK is chlamydia. The infection is caused by bacteria that can infect your cervix (the neck of your womb), urethra (the tube that carries urine from your bladder and out through your penis or vulva), rectum (back passage), throat or eyes.

'If you get infected with HPV, you may get warts on your genitals and anal area.'

About seven in ten infected women and half of infected men won't have any obvious signs or symptoms of chlamydia. If you do have signs or symptoms, these usually show up one to three weeks after being infected or may show many months later when the infection has spread to other parts of your body. Possible symptoms in women can include:

⇨ bleeding between periods or heavier periods

⇨ pain and/or bleeding during or after sex

⇨ lower abdominal pain

⇨ unusual vaginal discharge – such as a change in colour, texture or smell

⇨ pain when passing urine.

Symptoms in men can include:

⇨ a white, cloudy or watery discharge from the tip of the penis

⇨ pain when passing urine

⇨ pain in the testicles.

You may have symptoms in other areas of your body and some of these symptoms can be similar to other diseases, such as arthritis (joint pain). If you have an infection in your rectum, you may notice an unusual discharge from your anus and you may have pain there. You may get conjunctivitis, an inflammation of the transparent surface layer that covers the white of the eye (the conjunctiva).

Chlamydia can be treated with antibiotics. This may either be a single dose of an antibiotic or a course of antibiotics. If you have the signs and symptoms of chlamydia, you may be given treatment before your test results are back.

Genital warts

Genital warts, the second most common STI in the UK, are caused by infection with human papilloma virus (HPV). If you get infected with HPV, you may get warts on your genitals and anal area. Warts can vary in appearance. They can appear as small, smooth, round bumps or larger growths that are grouped together or small cauliflower-shaped bumps. Genital warts can also grow inside your urethra, vagina and anus. You can have HPV without having any symptoms, and you can pass on the virus even when you don't show any signs of having genital warts. Using condoms reduces the chances of you passing on the virus but, as the infected areas of skin might not be covered by a condom, this may not fully protect you or your partner against genital warts.

Although the warts may disappear on their own, you can be treated with a chemical solution or liquid nitrogen (cryotherapy) to remove them faster. Surgery or laser treatment are also options. You may need to have repeat treatment to get rid of the warts.

Genital herpes

Genital herpes is caused by the herpes simplex virus. Many people infected by this virus won't have any symptoms. If you do have symptoms, you may first notice stinging, tingling or itching in the genital or anal area followed by the development of fluid-filled blisters or sores on your genitals, anal area or tops of your thighs. You may also feel generally unwell, tired or have a fever.

The blisters will heal within about three weeks, but after the first 'primary' episode of genital herpes, you may have further outbreaks in the coming months. These outbreaks tend not to last as long or be as severe.

Another type of the virus causes oral herpes (cold sores). These can be passed to the genitals during oral sex. Genital herpes can also be passed to the mouth by oral sex.

'Gonorrhoea is caused by bacteria that can infect your urethra, cervix, rectum, mouth and throat'

There is no treatment that can completely remove the virus from your body, but you can be prescribed antiviral medicine by your GP that will help to clear up the blisters more quickly. You may be able to manage your symptoms by having salt baths and taking painkillers. You can have the virus but not show any symptoms and still pass the virus on to your partner. Using condoms can help to lower the chances of passing the virus on, but can't completely prevent this happening.

Gonorrhoea

Gonorrhoea is caused by bacteria that can infect your urethra, cervix, rectum, mouth and throat. You may have symptoms that appear up to 14 days after you become infected. However, one in ten men and half of all women who are infected have no symptoms.

In women, symptoms may include:

⇨ unusual vaginal discharge, which may be yellow or green

⇨ pain when passing urine

⇨ lower abdominal pain or tenderness (this is rare)

⇨ rarely, bleeding between periods or heavier periods.

In men, symptoms may include:

⇨ unusual discharge from the tip of the penis, which may be white, yellow or green

⇨ pain when passing urine

⇨ rarely, pain or tenderness in the testicles

⇨ inflammation of the foreskin (this is less common).

You may sometimes have other symptoms depending on where the infection is. If it's in your rectum, usually there aren't any symptoms but you may have anal pain, discomfort or discharge. If you have the infection in your throat, you usually won't have any symptoms.

It's important to be treated for gonorrhoea as the infection can cause serious long-term health problems including infertility. Gonorrhoea can be treated with antibiotics.

Hepatitis B

Hepatitis B virus causes hepatitis, which is an inflammation of your liver. If you have any symptoms, and not everyone does, these start about one to six months after you become infected. You may feel generally unwell with a sore throat, tiredness, joint pains and a loss of appetite. You may also feel sick or vomit. Your symptoms may be more severe and cause abdominal pain and yellowing of your skin and eyes (jaundice). Your skin may itch and your urine may become darker.

Most people will recover from hepatitis B without treatment, but if you don't clear the infection after six months, you will become a chronic carrier of the disease. Being a chronic carrier means you may have no symptoms and be unaware that you're infected, but

you can still pass the infection on to other people. A chronic illness is one that lasts a long time, sometimes for the rest of the affected person's life. When describing an illness, the term 'chronic' refers to how long a person has it, not to how serious a condition is. Being a chronic carrier means you will be at a greater risk of developing cirrhosis of the liver and liver cancer.

You may be treated for hepatitis B with medicines including antivirals or ones that help your immune system fight the disease. A vaccine is also available to prevent hepatitis B. If you haven't been vaccinated against hepatitis B and have been exposed to the virus through sexual contact with someone who has the virus, you can be given an injection (hepatitis B immunoglobulin) and an accelerated course of the vaccine. You would be given this treatment at a sexual health clinic. It works best if you are given this within 48 hours of exposure.

HIV

Human immunodeficiency virus (HIV) attacks your immune system. Many people infected with HIV have no signs and symptoms at all. About half of people who become infected with HIV will have flu-like symptoms within a few weeks of becoming infected.

There is currently no treatment that can get rid of HIV from your body. However, at specialist centres, you can be given a combination of antiretroviral medicines to reduce the level of HIV in your blood. These treatments are very effective and work best if started sooner rather than later. It's important to be treated for HIV to reduce your risk of having serious health complications later on. Even if you're taking antiretroviral medicines for HIV, you can still pass on the infection through unprotected sex. If you have had unprotected sex with someone who has HIV or is at high risk of having HIV, you will be offered the option of taking a month's course of antiretroviral medicines (this is called post-exposure prophylaxis) to lower the chances of

developing the infection. These work best if started as soon as possible after exposure. Accident and emergency departments and sexual health clinics are the best places to get post-exposure prophylaxis.

Pubic lice

Pubic lice (also known as crabs) are tiny insects that live in coarse body hair such as pubic hair but also chest and leg hair, beards, eyelashes and eyebrows. They don't live in hair on the head and are not the same as head lice.

You may notice the lice in your body hair, but they are very tiny and hard to see. Other signs include finding the brown eggs (nits) stuck to your body hair, or seeing black powdery spots in your underwear from the lice droppings. Pubic lice may make you itch.

You can treat a pubic lice infection with lotions or shampoos that you may need to use over your whole body or leave on for up to 12 hours.

Syphilis

Syphilis is caused by bacteria. The disease has three stages: primary, secondary and tertiary. The primary stage begins about two to three weeks after you are infected when one or more sores may appear. Commonly these develop on your penis, anus, in your vagina or rectum, in your mouth or on your lips.

The secondary stage begins a few weeks after the sores have healed. You may have symptoms including feeling generally unwell with flu-like symptoms and a rash. If you aren't treated for syphilis, you can develop the tertiary stage of the disease. This can cause serious health problems including problems with the nervous system and heart.

Syphilis can be treated with antibiotics.

November 2011

⇨ Content provided by Bupa. For more information visit www.bupa.co.uk/health.

Sexually transmitted infection rates soar among young

Gonorrhoea cases causing major concern as health agency warns under-25s failing to use condoms with new partners.

By Sarah Boseley

Sexually transmitted infections are soaring among young people failing to use condoms with new partners, the Heath Protection Agency warns. There is particular concern about the numbers of very young people contracting gonorrhoea. Over half of all new infections – 57% – are in the under-25s, said the HPA in its annual report for England. Gonorrhoea cases among girls increased sharply from the age of 15 to peak at the age of 18, said Dr Gwenda Hughes, head of STI surveillance. 'We have got high rates of infection in this population. In the older group it is much lower – particularly in women,' she said.

There is also major concern about

men who have sex with men – who may be gay or bisexual. The largest upsurge in new diagnoses in 2011 were among this group. Gonorrhoea cases increased by 61%, chlamydia by 48% and syphilis by 28%. Sexual health charities suggested the Government's policy of cutting funding for sexual health awareness campaigns could be a factor while the Department of Health said more people were coming forward to be tested.

'The data in young, heterosexual people and MSM is very concerning,' said Hughes. 'Too many people are practising unsafe sex. They are getting STIs and putting themselves at risk of longer-term problems, such as [in women] ectopic pregnancies and

tubal infertility. We think it is crucial that work to reduce STIs continues with a focus on at-risk groups.'

In 2011, the number of newly diagnosed STIs rose by 2%, totalling nearly 427,000 new cases and reversing the small decline seen in previous years.

While the Government believes that more and better testing is a factor in the overall rise, HPA experts said they were worried to see a downturn in the number of people coming for a chlamydia test. Dr Angie Bone, director of the HPA's national chlamydia screening programme, said the numbers of diagnoses had dropped from 154,000 in 2010 to 148,000 last year, which did not mean less chlamydia in the community but less testing. 'This is something we are very keen to reverse,' she said. Chlamydia is a very common infection that often has no symptoms, but left untreated it can cause infertility.

Sexually active young people and MSM are recommended to have a chlamydia test every year and whenever they change partners. MSM should also have an HIV test with the same frequency. 'The more partners you have, the greater the risk of getting an STI,' said Hughes. 'People should consider reducing the number of partners they have and reduce overlap in their sexual partnerships.'

Gonorrhoea is becoming a bigger worry because the drugs used to treat it are losing their effect. 'This is a global problem, not just a UK problem,' said Hughes. 'This bug has successfully managed to develop resistance to every treatment that has been used for it for a decade. We are running out of options for managing this infection. We are concerned in the future it will become very difficult to treat.'

UNSAFE SEX

There were 20,065 cases of gonorrhoea last year, which is a 25% rise on the 16,835 in the previous year and the biggest rise in any STI. Syphilis cases were up 10% from 2,650 to 2,915. Genital herpes and warts were also up by 5% and 1%, respectively. Chlamydia was down 2% from 189,314 to 186,196 cases.

There is concern that advertising campaigns and efforts to increase people's awareness of the risks of STIs have decreased. The last chlamydia awareness campaign, called 'Sex worth talking about', was in 2010. When the Coalition Government came to power, it temporarily froze all spending on social marketing, although funding for campaigns such as the anti-obesity drive Change4Life has resumed. The onus under the health reforms will now be on local authorities, who will be expected to champion the public health initiatives needed in their own area.

Sexual health charities FPA and Brook said in a joint statement that the rise in STIs is a worrying trend. 'It demonstrates exactly why safer sex messages and campaigns that young people and gay men will listen to and take action on, are absolutely necessary. Testing and treatment services are vital, but alone they are not enough to change people's behaviour.

'The impact of the Government's disinvestment in campaigning around safer sex and sexual health reflects in today's statistics. Yet again we see more data illustrating why there is an urgent need for statutory sex and relationships education in schools alongside sustained investment in sexual health services.'

A Department of Health spokesperson said: 'The fact that more people are coming forward to be tested and the improvements there have been in the way tests are done is to be welcomed.

But it's also clear that not enough people are taking care of their sexual health.

'Sexually transmitted infections can lead to infertility and other serious health problems. The message is clear: whatever your age, you should always use a condom.

'We are changing the way we deal with public health issues by giving local councils ring-fenced budgets so they can raise awareness of and improve sexual health in their communities.'

31 May 2012

⇨ The above article originally appeared in *The Guardian* and is reprinted with permission. Please visit www.guardian.co.uk for further information.

© Guardian News & Media Ltd 2012

Condoms: too embarrassed to buy them?

Extracts from YouGov Labs discussions.

Male participants who were not embarrassed to buy condoms

A recurring opinion emerged; buying condoms is a 'mark of pride', not something to be uncomfortable about:

'Why should the cashier care? I see it almost as a mark of pride' *Inverness*

'We all know what they are for, so why be embarrassed? We should be proud that we're having safe sex' *Robert Portland Dorset*

Male participants who were embarrassed to buy condoms

A small number of male participants said they were embarrassed to buy condoms. One reason was because they have experienced – or felt that people judge them:

'Because people sometimes give you dirty looks' *Anon*

To some participants buying condoms seemed like a public statement that one is planning to have sex, which is usually hidden:

'You are effectively saying to everyone who can see you, I plan on having sex. We usually hide this statement, or wrap it up with lots of jokes and euphemisms' *Anon*

Female participants who were not embarrassed to buy condoms

More female participants said they were not embarrassed to buy condoms, than embarrassed. Many believed that buying condoms is normal and that it doesn't actually imply that one is sleeping around:

'It's a normal thing, plus it's possible to be in a relationship and buy condoms regularly so it doesn't mean you're sleeping around. Not that the shop assistants care anyway' *Anon*

Females also outlined the health factor and said that buying condoms is the responsible thing to do. Unlike men participants, they seemed to mention the function of protecting from unplanned pregnancy more:

'I prefer buying condoms to getting pregnant and/or getting a disease' *Anon*

'It would be embarrassing if you caught a disease from not wearing one, so better safe than sorry!' *Una, Cardiff*

'I am not embarrassed as I think it should be looked upon as taking responsibility of unwanted child or risk of infection' *Sue*

Female participants who said they were embarrassed to buy condoms

Only a small number of female Labs participants said they were embarrassed to buy condoms. The main reason was feeling judged:

'As a female from an Asian background, I feel I will be judged by the sales person, the cashier and also the people around me' *Anon*

9 November 2012

⇨ Information from YouGov. www.yougov.co.uk.

© 2000-2012 YouGov plc

What is cervical cancer?

Information from NHS Choices.

Cervical cancer is an uncommon type of cancer that develops in a woman's cervix. The cervix is the entrance to the womb from the vagina.

Cervical cancer often has no symptoms in its early stages. If you have symptoms, the most common is unusual vaginal bleeding, which can occur after sex, in between periods or after the menopause.

Abnormal bleeding doesn't mean that you definitely have cervical cancer, but it's a cause for concern. It's important to see your GP as soon as possible. If your GP suspects you might have cervical cancer, you should be referred to see a specialist within two weeks.

'In the UK there were around 950 deaths due to cervical cancer in 2008.'

Screening for cervical cancer

Over the course of many years, the cells lining the surface of the cervix undergo a series of changes. In rare cases, these changed cells can become cancerous. However, cell changes in the cervix can be detected at a very early stage, and treatments can reduce the risk of cervical cancer developing.

The NHS offers a national screening programme for all women over 24 years old. During screening, a small sample of cells is taken from the cervix and checked under a microscope for abnormalities. This test is commonly referred to as a cervical smear test.

It is recommended that women who are between 25 and 49 years old are screened every three years, and women between 50 and 64 are screened every five years. You should be sent a letter telling you when your screening appointment is due. Contact your GP if you think that you may be overdue for a screening appointment.

Treating cervical cancer

If cervical cancer is diagnosed at an early stage, it's usually possible to treat it using surgery. In some cases, it's possible to leave the womb in place, but sometimes it will need to be removed. The surgical procedure that is used to remove the womb is known as a hysterectomy. Radiotherapy is an alternative to surgery for some women with early stage cervical cancer.

More advanced cases of cervical cancer are usually treated using a combination of chemotherapy and radiotherapy. Radiotherapy can also cause infertility as a side effect.

Causes of cervical cancer

Almost all cases of cervical cancer are caused by the human papilloma virus (HPV). HPV is a very common virus that's spread during sex. It's a common cause of genital warts.

There are more than 100 different types of HPV, many of which are harmless. However, some types of HPV can disrupt the normal functioning of the cells of the cervix. This causes them to reproduce uncontrollably and trigger the onset of cancer.

Two distinct strains of the HPV virus are known to be responsible for 70% of all cases of cervical cancer. They are HPV 16 and HPV 18. Most women who are infected with these two types of HPV are unaffected, which means that there must be additional factors that make some women more vulnerable to HPV infection than others.

HPV vaccination

In 2008, a national vaccination programme was launched to vaccinate girls against HPV 16 and HPV 18. The vaccine is most effective if it's given a few years before a girl becomes sexually active, so it's given to girls between the ages of 12 and 13.

The vaccine used is Gardasil – which provides protection against cervical cancer and genital warts

The vaccine protects against the two strains of HPV responsible for more than 70% of cervical cancers in the UK. However you should still attend your future screening appointments even if you have been vaccinated.

'The vaccine protects against the two strains of HPV responsible for more than 70% of cervical cancers in the UK.'

Complications of cervical cancer

Many women with cervical cancer will have complications. Complications can arise as a direct result of the cancer or as a side effect of treatments such as radiotherapy, surgery and chemotherapy.

Complications that are associated with cervical cancer can range from the relatively minor, such as minor bleeding from the vagina or having to urinate frequently, to being life-threatening, such as severe bleeding from the vagina or kidney failure.

Who is affected by cervical cancer?

Due to the success of the NHS screening programme, cervical cancer is now an uncommon type of cancer in the UK. However, it's still a common cause of cancer-related death in countries that don't offer screening.

It's possible for women of all ages to develop cervical cancer. However, the condition mainly affects sexually active women between 25 and 45 years old. Many women who are affected did not attend their screening appointments.

In 2007, nearly 2,800 cases of cervical cancer were diagnosed in the UK. In addition, about 25,000 cases were diagnosed with a pre-cancerous condition of the cervix called cervical intraepithelial neoplasia (CIN).

Outlook

The stage at which cervical cancer is diagnosed is an important factor in determining a woman's outlook. For example, if the cancer is still at an early stage, the outlook will usually be very good and a complete cure is often possible.

More than 90% of women with stage one cervical cancer will live at least five years after receiving a diagnosis. Many women will live much longer. Researchers used five years as a cut-off point because cancer is unlikely to recur after five years and most women can consider themselves cured after five years.

Around one in three people with the more advanced type of cervical cancer will live at least five years.

Another important factor is a woman's age when cervical cancer first develops. Older women usually have a worse outlook than younger women.

In the UK there were around 950 deaths due to cervical cancer in 2008.

4 October 2011

⇨ The above information is reprinted with kind permission from NHS Choices. Please visit www.nhs.uk for further information.

© NHS Choices 2011

Cervical cancer jab 'gives youngsters green light for promiscuity', charity LIFE says

An anti-abortion charity that advises the Government on sexual health has stirred controversy after pulling a statement on its website that said the cervical cancer jab 'gives young people another green light to be promiscuous'.

LIFE removed the controversial posting on its website after news that many school girls were being denied the jab, which protects against two strains of the human papilloma virus (HPV) that cause 70% of cases of cervical cancer, and is usually offered to girls aged 12-13.

It said: '[young people] do have choices about how they live their lives and the HPV vaccine suggests they won't be able to control themselves. We should have higher expectations for them and show them more respect, not vaccinate them en masse against STIs.'

However, the charity, which had used the message to back faith schools denying students the jab, said it still stood by its statement despite removing it.

Mark Bhagwandin told *The Huffington Post*: 'We still hold fast the comments that we made in that statement, it's just because we are looking at what we do as the media team in terms of what issues we speak on.'

Last week *GP* magazine had found 24 schools in 83 of England's 152 primary care trust (PCT) areas were opting out of the vaccination programme, many of them on religious grounds.

Labour's shadow public health minister Diane Abbott is now calling for Andrew Lansley to remove the group from the Department of Health's Sexual Health Forum, saying their views were 'staggering'.

'It's not good enough to just remove this statement from their website and pretend everything is OK again, because this group is closely advising Andrew Lansley on sexual health policy, and driving this Government's public health agenda,' she said.

'LIFE has an array of policy positions that I find staggering, and it is not suitable for this group to be advising the Government like this,' she said.

In a later statement, LIFE said: 'We wish to emphasise that LIFE was not directed to pull the press release on the HPV vaccine from our website. We decided to withdraw the release because we were concerned that it could be misconstrued or read out of context.

'All those involved in relationships and sex education should think very carefully about the messages being sent about sexual behaviour. For instance, we should be very aware of the danger of giving a false sense of security with measures like the HPV vaccine, which protects only against one particular STI and provides no protection against pregnancy.'

A Department of Health spokesperson told *The Huffington Post*: 'LIFE is one of the 11 groups that sit on the Sexual Health Forum. It is important to ensure that a wide range of views and interests are represented.

'The Sexual Health Forum does not advise on immunisation – this is provided by the independent Joint

New study reveals extent of Jade Goody effect on cervical screening

Information from NHS Cancer Screening Programmes.

Three years ago, Jade Goody died of cervical cancer. A new study, published today in the *Journal of Medical Screening*, discusses the effect of her death on cervical screening attendance. It showed that more than 400,000 extra women were screened in England between mid-2008 and mid-2009 – the period during which Jade Goody was diagnosed and died of cervical cancer.

More women of all ages were screened, though the increase was greater for women aged under 50. In the 25-29 age group, an estimated 31,000 extra women were screened in the five months between autumn 2008 and spring 2009. It seems that the women who were closest to Jade Goody in age or circumstances,

that is young women with young families, were those most affected by her experience.

Although there was concern that the increase in attendance might have been from the 'worried well' coming back for an early repeat screen, the research found that the opposite was true. A higher proportion was from women who were late for their test, rather than those who were coming back early. In the 25-49 age group, for example, 82,000 (28 per cent) women had not been tested for five years or longer, while only 7,500 (eight per cent) were coming back early having already been screened in the past three years.

Professor Julietta Patnick, Director of the NHS Cancer Screening Programmes, commented;

'Jade's tragic diagnosis and death played a huge role in raising awareness of cervical cancer and prompted a welcome increase in screening attendance in 2008/2009. Many of those women will now be due their next routine appointment and we would like to see them return.

'All women between the ages of 25 and 64 are eligible for free cervical screening every three to five years. Regular screening means that changes in the cervix which may develop into cancer can be identified and treated. Screening saves lives, and we would encourage all eligible women to consider attending a screening appointment when invited.

'It is important to remember, however, that cervical screening is aimed at women without symptoms. Women of any age with symptoms (for example, bleeding between periods or after intercourse) should contact their GP or genito-urinary medicine (GUM) clinic who will refer them to see an expert in hospital.'

1 June 2012

⇨ The above information is reprinted with kind permission from NHS Cancer Screening Programmes. Please visit www.cancerscreening.nhs.uk for further information.

Sex education

The UK still has a worryingly high teenage pregnancy rate, and sexually transmitted infections are also on the rise. Is sex education – or the lack of it – in schools to blame? We look at the facts of life...

By Kia Henson

There's something wrong with sex education in this country. There must be. The results speak for themselves. The highest number of teenage pregnancies in the whole of Western Europe (45, 873 in 2008). 20,000 girls under 18 undergoing an abortion last year. And high numbers of sexually transmitted infections (STIs); recent figures show 15- to 24-year-olds are still the group most affected by STIs in the UK. Dr Gwenda Hughes, head of the Health Protection Agency's STI section, says: 'The impact of STI diagnoses is still unacceptably high in this group. Studies suggest those infected may be more likely to have unsafe sex or lack the skills and confidence to negotiate safer sex.' Perhaps the 'relationships' aspect of Sex and Relationships Education (SRE) is seriously lacking.

Results from a campaign called Let's Talk About Sex, set up by 18-year-old Shereece Marcantonio, indicate that 40% of young people believe their sex education was poor. Shereece's campaign, run in conjunction with Channel 4's *Battlefront*, Campaigners on a Mission (www.battlefront.co.uk/sex) aims for a change in the way sex education is taught in schools: this young woman, whose three siblings all became teenage parents, wants to establish peer-to-peer sex education in schools, whereby young people are trained up to become educators so they can teach each other about sex. Her mission? To ensure young people can 'get the facts they need without the cringe'. She wants this vital subject taught 'in a language that teenagers all understand' – and to reverse the UK's shocking teen pregnancy, STI and abortion rates. Shereece is now a qualified sex and relationships educator who delivers lessons to secondary school children in east London and Essex. Shereece adds: 'It's all got to be about safe sex.'

Where does the problem lie?

A brief (and very unofficial) vox pop on SRE highlighted several issues. 'Traumatised.' One mum's analysis of her son's reaction to his first SRE lesson in Year Five. 'Terrified.' Another mum's description of her ten-year-old daughter's reaction to a video of a live birth. 'Outdated and corny.' A teacher's verdict of the video used in her lesson. 'It scared me and made me not want to use any. We were just told all about the bad side effects.' One teenage girl's opinion after a Year Nine lesson about contraception. 'Strange and vague.' A teenage girl's response to seeing a cartoon on the subject at primary school. And secondary school, where it's part of PSHE (Personal, Social, Health and Economic Education) was no better for her: 'Totally forgettable PowerPoint slides.'

It's little wonder, then, that guest editor Dr Christian considers sex education 'shoddy', and blames it for our poor sexual health.

SRE is, shockingly, not compulsory in schools. All schools are required to have a policy on it, but that policy could, in fact, be not to teach it. Brook (www.brook.org.uk), a charity that provides free, confidential advice to people under 25, says children face a 'lottery' over how much SRE they are taught. Statistics from Brook show that one in four children get no SRE at all. And of those that do, 80% say they 'have no voice in what they learn'. Even in lessons given, young people say they 'don't learn enough about emotions and relationships'. The figures also show that 36% of children claim to learn the most from friends their own age – which means it could be inaccurate – and, most worrying of all, a mere 7% claim to learn from their parents.

Models to learn from

Perhaps UK teachers, and parents, need to learn a few lessons from the Dutch. The Netherlands has the lowest rate of teenage pregnancy in Europe. Sex education in Holland is not required to follow a national curriculum, so teachers are able to teach about sex in many different ways. Indeed, Shereece's *Battlefront* study revealed that 'pupils empathise better with a more creative approach to sex and relationships education'. Parents back up school education, too – the country's culture of tolerance and pragmatism allows children to talk openly about sexuality with their parents at home. Scenes of British families discussing sex over the dinner table are, sadly, a long way off. Sex is still regarded as taboo when it comes to family conversation.

In addition, the Dutch approach has a heavy focus on empowerment and respect – put simply, the importance of being able to say, 'no'. We're not talking abstinence, but how to deal with pressure. Teaching looks at the seriousness of sex in relation to consent, the significance of first sexual intercourse and, crucially, potential pregnancy.

Findings from the UK Data Archive's *National Survey of Sexual Attitudes and Lifestyles* revealed that, of those surveyed, one in five young men and almost half of young women between the ages of 16 and 24 wished they had waited longer to start having sex. Anyone who had intercourse under the age of 15 was twice as likely to wish they'd waited. With today's figures,

it seems it's a case of after the horse has bolted…

Sweden follows a similar style of sex education to Holland. Lessons start from the age of six – covering anatomy, eggs and sperm; from age 12, the focus moves to disease, contraception, moral issues and gender equality. And it works: teen pregnancies, seven per 1,000 births, and STI rates are both among the world's lowest.

Nurse-led lessons

Do children feel more engaged when taught by a healthcare professional?

An interesting fact was revealed in the *Battlefront* research – 48% of girls said they'd like to be taught by a doctor or nurse (compared to 38% of boys).

From our own vox pop, Amy, 16, said: 'When our school nurse came to talk to us, it was more useful and interesting than when the teacher taught us. She knew much more

on the topic and interacted with the class – she mainly talked about sexual health and contraception. It was easier having someone who was more like a visitor, and she chatted with us on a more personal level. Without her, I wouldn't have learnt so much and I felt more comfortable asking her questions.'

But comments from Grace, 14, who also had nurse-led lessons, still favour 'age' over 'medical knowledge': 'In Year Nine we had a lesson about contraception and pregnancy. That wasn't very good at all. We had a nurse in but it would have been much better if it was a younger woman who we could relate to; I would have felt more comfortable and would have asked about more things I was unsure about.'

Shereece adds: 'Peer educators are not trying to replace teachers, but combined together, perhaps with sexual health services and doctor or nurse-led classes, there would be a fantastic compilation of quality SRE.' One simple fact can't be contested. We learn more when we like the way we're being taught. For that reason alone, a change in sex education can't come soon enough. Perhaps creativity is core: bin the slide shows and start thinking carrots and condoms. That might be food for thought.

If you want to show your support for Shereece's campaign, go to www.battlefront.co.uk/sex to add your name to her campaign. As we went to print, there were currently 4,580 supporters. Or visit www. brook.co.uk and sign its petition for the Government, demanding 21st Century Sex and Relationships Education.

4 April 2012

⇨ The above information is reprinted with kind permission from EMP PLC. Originally published in *At Home* magazine (www.athomemagazine.co.uk).

UK sex and relationships education fails to prepare young people for modern day life

Information from Brook.

Almost half (47%) of today's secondary school pupils say Sex and Relationships Education (SRE) doesn't cover what they really need to know about sex.

The information void this creates isn't filled by parents – only 5% of young people get their information from their mum and 1% from their dad.

82% of young people say schools should listen to young people when shaping SRE.

New research released today shows 47% of secondary school pupils think their school's Sex and Relationships Education (SRE) does not meet their needs. The lack of relevant sex and relationships education in schools and at home means 81% of teenagers are getting most of their sexual health knowledge from less reliable sources, leaving them vulnerable and ill-prepared to navigate their way through relationships.

The study of over 2,000 14-18-year-olds, commissioned by Brook, the country's largest young people's sexual health charity illustrates the impact on young people that the country's lack of commitment to good Sex and Relationships Education, out of date guidelines for schools and a lack of support for well qualified teachers is having.

The survey finds that young people rely on often ill-informed sources, such as peers, for information resulting in the spread of dangerous sex myths which can lead to poor decisions and unwanted outcomes. The five most commonly shared sex myths amongst peers are:

⇨ 59% of young people have wrongly heard from their friends that a woman cannot get pregnant if the man withdraws before he ejaculates.

⇨ 58% of young people have wrongly heard that women cannot get pregnant if they are having their period.

⇨ 35% have wrongly heard that women cannot get pregnant if they have sex standing up.

⇨ 33% have wrongly heard from their friends that a woman cannot get pregnant if it is the first time she has had sex.

⇨ 25% of young people have wrongly heard that you can only catch HIV from gay sex.

Schools are not required to consult with their pupils to shape SRE lessons, and 78% of young people confirm they have never been consulted. As the Government recently announced a review of Personal, Social, Health and Economic Education (PSHE), 82% of young people said they want schools to take their views into account to help make SRE relevant for the 21st century.

The research identified the scale of the SRE problem:

⇨ One in four (26%) secondary pupils get no SRE in school whatsoever.

⇨ A quarter (26%) of those who do get SRE say the teacher isn't able to teach it well.

⇨ Only 13% of 14-18-year-olds learn most about sex from their SRE teacher, and just 5% from Mum and 1% from dad at home.

⇨ The sex information void is being filled by friends their own age (36%), their boyfriend/girlfriend (10%), TV programmes (8%) and online porn (5%) – none of which are reliable sources of honest, useful information.

⇨ SRE fares particularly badly when it comes to teaching pupils about relationships, with only 6% saying they get the information on relationships that they need in SRE lessons.

In light of this research, Brook is launching the 'Say YES to 21st Century Sex and Relationships Education' campaign to give today's teenagers their say on how they want to be taught SRE and what they want to learn, as part of its wider Sex:Positive work. Over the next seven weeks, Brook will gather the views of thousands more young people and present its resulting report to the Department for Education, ahead of the submissions deadline for its review into SRE as part of PSHE.

Jules Hillier, Brook Deputy Chief Executive, says:

'Young people in Britain deserve honest, useful information about sex and relationships but SRE in UK schools is failing them. Standards vary so widely that all too often young people miss out on the information they need to stay safe, healthy and happy. Worse, we know that the void is not being filled by reliable information from elsewhere – like parents – but from the playground and, even more worrying, Internet porn.

'Learning about sex and relationships is a crucial life skill and by letting teenagers leave school ill-informed we are letting them down. We are calling on young people to seize the opportunity to make their voices heard by telling us what they think 21st century SRE should cover, to better meet their needs.'

Yessica, Brook volunteer said:

'My school didn't offer SRE classes until Year 11, when I was 15 going on 16, by which time I was pregnant so it was too late. I wasn't allowed to take part in the lessons as the teacher said it wouldn't be relevant for me, so I had to look elsewhere for information which was often incorrect.

'I do not blame my school for my decisions but if I was taught SRE sooner and had been given honest, accurate information when I needed it, I would have had a different mentality and would have made different choices. That is why Brook's "Say YES to 21st Century Sex and Relationships Education" campaign is so important to me.'

To support Brook's 'Say YES to 21st Century Sex and Relationships Education' campaign sign up to the petition here: http://www.change. org/petitions/uk-parliament-support-21st-century-sex-and-relationship-education.

Notes

The 'Say YES to 21st Century Sex and Relationships Education' campaign is supported by music group, JLS.

Aston from JLS says: 'I agree that UK sex education could definitely go further to meet the needs of young people today. Teens in Britain deserve more honest, useful information about sex and relationships. Learning about relationships is as important as the basic biology lesson. I wish I had had the opportunity to ask exactly what I wanted to about sex when I was at school, in the end I just chatted to my friends whose answers were not always correct!'

Oritsé from JLS says: 'Brook's new campaign is a great platform to allow young people to actually have their say on what they really want out of their sex education classes. Make sure you sign the Brook 'Say YES to 21st Century Sex and Relationships Education' e-petition!'

For more information about the campaign, please visit http://www. brook.org.uk/sex-positive.

Show support of the 'Say YES to 21st Century Sex and Relationships Education' campaign via Twitter, using the hashtags #sexednevertaughtme and #whatsexedtaughtme.

Research

All figures quoted in the release are from ResearchBods (formerly Dubit) 'Direct to Youth' research panel. Total sample size was 2,029 14-18-year-olds and the figures are representative of all young people in the UK. All panel members under the age of 16 have the express verbal and recorded consent of their parent or guardian to participate. Fieldwork was undertaken between 14-28 September 2011.

12 October 2011

⇨ The above information is reprinted with kind permission from Brook. Please visit www.brook.org.uk for further information.

© *Brook*

Notes

Brook helps young people to make informed, active choices about their personal and sexual relationships so they can enjoy their sexuality without harm.

Brook is the UK's leading provider of sexual health services and advice for young people under 25. The charity has over 45 years of experience working with young people and currently has services in England, Scotland, Northern Ireland and Jersey.

Brook services provide free and confidential sexual health information, contraception, pregnancy testing, advice and counselling, testing and treatment for sexually transmitted infections and outreach and education work, reaching over 260,000 young people every year.

The Ask Brook information service offers a confidential helpline, online enquiry service and interactive text message service. Ask Brook is available free and in confidence to young people on 0808 802 1234 or via www.askbrook.org.uk.

Brook's Sex:Positive campaign aims to challenge society's negative attitudes towards sex. Join the campaign: www.sexpositive.org.uk.

Follow us on Twitter: @BrookCharity @BeSexPositive

Explicit sex education website condemned as 'grossly irresponsible'

NHS and council officials have been accused of 'condoning' sexual experimentation among under-age teenagers after creating a website and mobile phone app featuring explicit sex tips for children as young as 13.

By Sam Marsden

The free online service features pictures of a naked man and woman with their erogenous zones highlighted, a 'sextionary' including definitions of slang terms for genitalia, and a question-and-answer section covering a variety of sexual acts.

A family charity said the Respect Yourself website, which is modelled on the more liberal Dutch approach to sex education, was 'grossly irresponsible' and encouraged an 'unhealthy obsession with physical acts'.

The Internet site and smartphone app, the first of their kind in Britain, are aimed at children 13 and over, and were created by a team from Warwickshire County Council working with NHS Warwickshire and Coventry University.

An FAQ section features answers to questions posed by teenagers ranging from 'What is the most common age to lose your virginity?' to 'Where can I buy the *Kama Sutra*?'.

In response to the question, 'Why do you have to be 16 to have sex? What if you want it now?', the website states: 'The law says you are not old enough to decide for yourself until you are 16 – as this is the age the law sees us as being mature enough to decide. You are the only one who knows when you are ready. Some are ready before, some not till much later.'

Young people thinking about losing their virginity are directed to a page entitled 'Am I Ready?' with a list of six questions designed to help them decide.

The £24,000 cost of developing the site and app came from an NHS West Midlands research fund.

Norman Wells, director of the Family Education Trust, a national charity, claimed that the website only 'paid lip service' to the legal age of consent, adding: 'It pretty much tells young people they can engage in sexual activity whenever they feel ready, regardless of what the law says.'

He went on: 'Parents throughout the region will be appalled that health professionals have supported the development of a resource that condones sexual experimentation by young people and uses crude and sometimes even foul language.

'This is a grossly irresponsible website and a complete misuse of taxpayers' hard-earned cash.

'Many of the topics covered are totally unnecessary and positively unhelpful. Young people – and older people for that matter – simply don't need a 'sextionary' containing an A-Z of all manner of sexual practices and perversions.

'It merely encourages an unhealthy obsession with physical acts and will do nothing to help young people build healthy relationships or prepare them for a stable and fulfilling marriage in the future.

'Not only does the site include a considerable volume of unhealthy and unhelpful content, but much of the information provided is not even accurate.'

The website's developers used research from a European-funded study tour of the Netherlands, where sex education for young people focuses on pleasure as well as biological facts.

Amy Danahay, project manager of Respect Yourself, said: 'The Internet has changed how young people find out about sex.

'It would be naïve to think that many young people are not regularly accessing far more explicit material and if we want to give them access to relevant information, we have to move with the times – 53 per cent of ten-year-olds have accessed some kind of porn on the Internet.

'It is far better that we provide accurate information for them which is easily accessible and monitored by professionals.

'We have involved young people throughout the development about how best to reach them and communicate with them. We have used language that young people understand and use. The app has been based on thorough research into what young people need, how they want to access the information and how it should be presented.

'It is based on research into how this information is presented in Holland where the rate of teenage pregnancy is over five times lower than it is in England and where contraception is much more widely used. Clearly their approach has worked and we would be wrong if we neglected to take lessons from that.'

24 October 2012

⇨ The above article originally appeared in *The Telegraph* and is reprinted with permission. Please visit www.telegraph.co.uk for further information.

Sex education: we should teach young people about more than the mechanics

Young people need comprehensive sexuality education, which will help them make more informed decisions.

By Doortje Braeken

Sex education polarises opinion, sets legislators against parents and parents against schools and regularly inflames media opinion. Somewhere in the middle sit young people: ill-served, receiving confused messages and gaining their information from famously unreliable sources, such as peers or the Internet.

Sex education, as all too many experience it, is like teaching people how to drive by telling them in detail what's under the bonnet, how the bits work, how to maintain them safely to avoid accidents, what the controls do and when to go on the road. It's all about the mechanics. And that's it.

There's a growing consensus that young people don't need sex education, they need comprehensive sexuality education (CSE). CSE is sex education plus: the mechanics, plus a lots more about sexuality.

That means not just teaching young people about the biology of sex, but also teaching them about the personal, emotional, societal and cultural forces which shape the way in which they choose to conduct their lives. Armed with this understanding, young people can make far more considered decisions.

This approach has the potential to unite the warring factions that bicker over the fundamental rights and wrongs of sex education: CSE equips young people with basic biological knowledge, but at the same time it equips them to question why they act in certain ways, and whether or not it is right, valuable or desirable to do so. CSE imparts information, and promotes responsibility.

CSE contains components which allow learners to explore and discuss gender, and the diverse spectrum of gender identities that exist within and between and beyond simple heterosexuality. It also contains components that examine the dynamics of power in relationships, and individual rights.

These are not taught as theoretical concepts. They have serious practical effects on the way in which young people interact with each other, both in the sexual and the wider social and educational spheres. Studies have shown that addressing such issues can have a marked impact both in school and the expansion of young people's social networks.

CSE also engages with what some doubtless regard as difficult territory. Sexuality – however, individually, we choose to regard it – is a critical aspect of personal identity. The pleasure that we derive from sexuality, even if that pleasure is the pleasure of feeling that a reproductive duty is being fulfilled, is a vital part of our lives: it's what makes us human. CSE views sexuality as a positive force.

CSE exploits a variety of teaching and learning techniques that are respectful of age, experience and cultural backgrounds, and which engage young people by enabling them to personalise the information they receive.

What is most telling is that a large number

of studies have reached the clear conclusion that CSE does not lead to earlier sexual initiation or an increase in sexual activity. To paraphrase, traditional sex education seems to say: 'If you're going to do it, this is how everything works and you need to protect yourself in these ways to prevent this.' CSE says all that, but it also asks young people to ponder what exactly 'it' is, and to deepen their perception of its implications.

In a political environment which is quantitatively driven, we measure the success of sex education in straightforward health behaviour indicators. These are easy to manage: numbers which build on existing health surveillance and measurement systems, and which are simple to understand from an objective point of view.

However, CSE is a far more nuanced discipline, and it will be necessary to include other measures of programme success: qualitative, subjective indicators which relate to gender equity, empowerment and critical thinking skills.

While governments have recognised young people's right to CSE via various intergovernmental resolutions and conventions, the journey from recognition to delivery will be a long one. Even in the UK, there are notable differences, with England having a bare-bones biological approach 'puberty, menstruation, contraception, abortion, safer sex, HIV/Aids and STIs should be covered', while Wales and Scotland have curriculums which incline far more towards the CSE agenda.

The International Planned Parenthood Federation, the organisation I work for, and its 153 member associations around the world, has been instrumental in pressing for the adoption of international policy commitments to CSE. For many, it may seem like we are pushing ten steps ahead of the agenda when the basic principle of young people's right to even the most basic introduction to the biology of sex is still not universally accepted.

Our view is different: it is that CSE is what will secure widespread acceptance of sex education, because it is about more than the mechanics of sex. It is about helping young people the world over to become more healthy, more informed, more respectful and more active participants in the life of their community and their nation.

24 May 2012

⇨ The above information originally appeared in *The Guardian* and is reprinted with permission. Please visit www.guardian.co.uk for further information.

© Guardian News & Media Ltd 2012

Teenagers want sex education from their peers, study finds

Young people are turning to friends for sex and relationships (SRE) education because teachers 'come up short', latest research has found.

By Neil Puffett

A ComRes survey of schools around Britain for Channel 4 shows half of 13- to 17-year-olds questioned (49 per cent) felt they had received too little SRE in their schools.

The majority of pupils (56 per cent) said they are most likely to learn about sex from their friends. And 82 per cent of the 1,123 questioned wanted sex and relationships education to come from a trained young person.

The survey suggests current SRE lessons are not meeting young people's needs. The Government is due to publish an Internal review of personal, social, health and economic education on 30 November.

The poll found that half (49 per cent) of pupils felt awkward asking questions in SRE lessons taught by teachers – only one in five felt comfortable asking questions.

But 67 per cent of pupils said they would be comfortable asking questions to a trained young person.

In total 70 per cent wanted to receive more SRE lessons taught by a trained young person compared to three per cent who didn't.

Shereece Marcantonio, an 18-year-old peer sex and relationships educator from east London, has been campaigning for teenagers to be taught by trained older teenagers.

She said: 'My campaign has always been about changing the national curriculum, by trying to get peer-to-peer teaching of sex and relationship education.

'If we can educate kids in a relaxed and engaging way, we can help avoid unwanted pregnancies and help teenagers cope with their first sexual experiences safely.'

16 November 2011

⇨ The above information is reprinted with kind permission from Children and Young People Now. Please visit www.cypnow.co.uk for further information.

© MA Business & Leisure Limited 2012

Key facts

⇨ There is also a form of contraception called the emergency contraception pill, which can help prevent unintended pregnancy. It can be taken by girls within 72 hours after unprotected sex, although preferably with 24 hours. It is available across the counter at chemists or from your local GP, family planning clinic or sexual health clinic. (page 2)

⇨ There's a myth that a girl can't get pregnant if she has sex during her period. The truth is, she can get pregnant at any time of the month if she has sex without contraception. (page 3)

⇨ The male condom is 98% effective if it is used according to instructions. This means that two women in 100 will get pregnant in a year. (page 6)

⇨ If 100 sexually active women don't use any contraception, 80 to 90 will become pregnant in a year. (page 6)

⇨ In Brazil and Indonesia, where there is limited sex education, as many as 67% and 48% of young people have a close friend of family member who has had an unplanned pregnancy. Furthermore, in France and Norway, where 85% and 84% of young people receive sex education, only 25% and 24%, know a close friend or family member who has had an unplanned pregnancy. (page 8)

⇨ 44% of young people prioritise personal hygiene, including showering, waxing and applying perfume, above contraception when preparing for a date that may lead to sex. (page 9)

⇨ If unmet need for contraception was fully satisfied, each year 53 million more unintended pregnancies could be prevented. (page 10)

⇨ 15% of young adults between the ages of 18 and 26 have had a sexually transmitted disease in the past year. (page 10)

⇨ Having sex without gaining consent could potentially lead to you spending up to eight years in prison. (page 13)

⇨ The results of the 2011 Young Life and Times survey show that nearly three quarters of 16-year-olds had not had sex. Among those who did, almost half said having sex for them was a natural follow-on in the relationship they were in at the time. (page 17)

⇨ The best way to avoid STIs is to use a condom every time you have sex. (page 18)

⇨ The most common STI in the UK is chlamydia. About seven in ten infected women and half of infected men won't have any obvious signs or symptoms of chlamydia. (page 20)

⇨ A new survey from The Site.org revealed that 16- to 25-year-olds have a worrying lack of concern about the dangers of STIs, with almost half (47%) of respondents agreeing that it's OK to have sex without a condom, providing the girl is on the pill. (page 23)

⇨ In 2008, a national vaccination programme was launched to vaccinate girls against HPV 16 and HPV 18. The vaccine is most effective if it's given a few years before a girl becomes sexually active, so it's given to girls between the ages of 12 and 13. The vaccine used is Gardasil – which provides protection against cervical cancer and genital warts. The vaccine protects against the two strains of HPV responsible for more than 70% of cervical cancers in the UK. (page 28)

⇨ Approximately 1,000 women in the UK die each year from cervical cancer. (page 31)

⇨ Almost half (47%) of today's secondary school pupils say Sex and Relationships Education (SRE) doesn't cover what they really need to know about sex. (page 35)

Cervical cancer

Cancer that develops in a woman's cervix (the entrance to the womb from the vagina). In its early stages it often has no symptoms. Symptoms can include unusual vaginal bleeding which can occur after sex, in between periods or after menopause. The NHS offers a national screening programme; a 'smear test' for all women over 24 years old.

Condoms

A thin rubber (latex) sleeve worn on the penis. When used correctly, condoms are the only form of contraception that protect against pregnancy AND STIs. They are 98% effective – this means that two out of 100 women using male condoms as contraception will become pregnant in one year. You can get free condoms from sexual health clinics and some GP surgeries.

Contraception

Sometimes called birth control, contraception is a way to prevent pregnancy. Some forms of contraception, but not all, help reduce the spread of STIs. Contraception is a very important part of making sure sex is safe and taking responsibility for your actions. There are many different types of contraception available; such as the pill, condoms, diaphragms, contraceptive implant (e.g. Implanon) and contraceptive injections.

Contraceptive implant

A small flexible tube about the size of a matchstick inserted by a doctor under the skin of a female's upper arm. The device releases hormones to prevent the ovaries from releasing eggs. Lasts for three years, but can be removed before then if the woman decided she wants to get pregnant.

Contraceptive injections

An injection offers eight to 12 weeks protection against pregnancy, but not from sexually transmitted diseases (approx. 99% effective). It works by thickening the mucus in the cervix, which stops sperm reaching the egg, and it also thins the lining of the womb so that an egg can't implant itself there.

Diaphragms

A rubber dome-shaped device worn inside the vagina which creates a seal against the walls of the vagina. It must be inserted before sexual intercourse and must remain in places for up to six to eight hours afterwards. The diaphragm does not provide protection from sexually transmitted diseases.

Emergency contraception

Sometimes referred to as the 'morning-after pill', this is a form of emergency contraception which can be taken by girls within 72 hours after unprotected sex (although preferably within the first 24 hours). It should not be used as a regular method of contraceptive. It is available across the counter at chemists or from your local GP, family planning clinic or sexual health clinic.

Femidom

Female condom: used by the female partner to provide a physical barrier that prevents sperm from reaching the egg. Can help prevent pregnancy and reduce the risk of STIs.

HPV vaccination

An injection for girls which can help prevent cervical cancer and genital warts. The vaccine protects against the two strains of HPV (human papilloma virus) responsible for more than 70% of cervical cancers in the UK. It is most effective a few years before a girl becomes sexually active. A national vaccination programme launched in 2008 to vaccinate 12- and 13-year-old girls.

Safe sex

Being safe with sex means caring for both your own health, and the health of your partner. Being safe protects you from getting or passing on STIs and from unplanned pregnancy.

Sexual health

Taking care of your sexual health means more than being free from sexually transmissible infections (STIs) or not having to face an unplanned pregnancy. It also means taking responsibility for your body, your health, your partner's health and your decisions about sex.

Sexually transmitted infections (STIs / STDs)

A sexually transmitted infection (STIs), also referred to as sexually transferred diseases (STDs), is a bacterial or viral infection that is spread through sexual contact. This doesn't just mean vaginal/anal sexual intercourse, but also oral sex (licking/sucking on someone's genitals) and sexual touching (skin-to-skin contact). Using condoms are the best way of avoiding STIs. Although STIs are treatable, if left unchecked and untreated they may cause serious damage to long-term health, such as infertility. The most common STI in the UK is chlamydia.

The pill

A tablet taken each day, at the same time, by girls to prevent pregnancy. The pill contains hormones that prevent the ovaries from releasing an egg. It only protects against pregnancy and not STIs.

Assignments

1. Create an informative leaflet about the different kinds of sexually transmitted infections (STIs), including how they are passed on, symptoms and how to treat them.

2. In groups, design a storyboard for a series of YouTube videos that will promote the use of contraception amongst young people.

3. Chlamydia is the most common sexually transmitted infection amongst young people. Create an informative presentation on the signs and symptoms of chlamydia, the risks associated with it and how somebody can request a free test kit.

4. 'I won't get pregnant if we have sex standing up' is a common myth that many of us may have heard. What other sexual health related myths have you heard that need busting? Discuss in pairs or small groups, then read '15 things you should know about sex' on page 3 and 'Contraception myths' on page 11. Compare your answers (note: these articles are not a list of ALL the myths and facts regarding sex, only a small selection).

5. Draw a cartoon strip about how to put on and use a condom correctly that would be suitable to be used in sex education lessons for your age-group.

6. Imagine you are a journalist for your local newspaper, read 'New survey reveals young people are unaware of STI risks' on page 23 and write a summary of the article's findings.

7. Your friend has been dating his girlfriend for several months and he has confided in you that he thinks that they are both ready to have sex. Although he is over 16, she is not. He explains that it will be okay because she has given him sexual consent. How do you respond? What do you think he should do?

8. What is the definition of rape? Look at sex and the law in the UK. What are the possible consequences of sex or physical closeness without consent? Consider not just the legal impact, but the health and emotional effects too. Write a summary of your findings.

9. Your friend Jenny has confided in you that, although her partner does not physically force her, she feels pressured into performing sexual acts that she isn't sure about. Although in the past she has consented to having sex, even when she says no they sometimes have sex anyway. How do you respond to Jenny? What advice would you give her?

10. In 2008, a national vaccination programme was launched to vaccinate girls against HPV 16 and HPV 18. Conduct some research and gather information on the HPV vaccination programme and the vaccine itself. Here are a few questions to get you started: What does the vaccine do? Are there any negative side effects or problems? Can males be given the HPV injection?

11. 'Almost half (47%) of today's secondary school pupils say Sex and Relationships Education (SRE) doesn't cover what they really need to know about sex.' ('UK sex and relationships education fails to prepare young people for modern day life' on page 35). Do you agree? How do you feel about the sex education you received at school? How could it be improved upon?

12. Plan a sex education class to be taught to ten- to 12-year olds. What information would you include? What information would you leave out? Who would be best to teach the class (e.g. a younger woman, an experienced nurse, a teacher, a parent)?

13. At what age should sex education be taught? How young is too young? Debate this as a group.

14. Read 'New study reveals extent of Jade Goody effect on cervical screening.' on page 32. What is the 'Jade Goody effect'? What effect did it have on cervical screening? Using this information, create your own cervical cancer awareness campaign. Use the Internet to see if there are any campaigns currently running and look at sexual health awareness campaigns for inspiration too.

15. Sexual health is not just all about STIs; it should also include a respectful understanding of sex and the mental and emotional aspects involved. Make a list of all the things a person should consider before having sexual intercourse.

16. Design a leaflet that will be given to parents of teenage children, offering hints and tips on how they should approach talking about sex and sexual health with their teenager.

Acknowledgements

The publisher is grateful for permission to reproduce the following material.

While every care has been taken to trace and acknowledge copyright, the publisher tenders its apology for any accidental infringement or where copyright has proved untraceable. The publisher would be pleased to come to a suitable arrangement in any such case with the rightful owner.

Chapter One: What is sexual health?

What is sexual health? © The State of Queensland (Queensland Health) 2010, 15 things you should know about sex © NHS Choices 2011, Sexual health quiz © Bedfordshire PCT, Questions and answers about contraception © 2012 University of Oxford, 'Clueless or clued up: your right to be informed about contraception' media report © Bayer HealthCare Pharmaceuticals, Contraception myths © 2012 Whittall Street Clinic, Sexual consent and the law © Crown copyright 2012, Messed up? © 2012 ARK.

Chapter Two: STIs, HPV and cancer

All about STIs © Brook, Types of STIs © Bupa 2011, Chlamydia © test.me 2010, New survey reveals young people are unaware of STI risks © 2012 YouthNet, Sexually transmitted infection rates soar among young © Guardian News & Media Ltd 2012, Condoms: too embarrassed to buy them? © 2000-2012 YouGov plc, HPV vaccines © Cancer Research UK, What is cervical cancer? © NHS Choices 2011, Cervical cancer jab 'gives youngsters green light for promiscuity', charity LIFE says © 2012 AOL (UK) Limited, Life-saving vaccine denied to girls © Education for Choice 2012, New study reveals extent of Jade Goody effect on cervical screening © 2000 – 2012 NHS Cancer Screening Programmes.

Chapter Three: Sex education

Sex education © 2009-2012 EMP PLC, UK sex and relationships education fails to prepare young people for modern day life © Brook, Explicit sex education website condemned as 'grossly irresponsible' © Telegraph Media Group Limited 2012, Sex education: we should teach young people about more than the mechanics © Guardian News & Media Ltd 2012, Teenagers want sex education from their peers, study finds © MA Business & Leisure Limited 2012.

Illustrations:

Pages 24, 30: Don Hatcher; pages 18, 38: Angelo Madrid; pages 26, 34: Simon Kneebone.

Images:

Cover: © Dan Comaniciu, page 5 © Pixels Away, page 6 © Julien Tromeur, page 11 © Joe Cicack, page 12 © gabuchia, page 21 © Mark Wragg, page 32 © Keira76, page 35 © CactuSoup.

Additional acknowledgements:

Editorial on behalf of Independence Educational Publishers by Cara Acred.

With thanks to the Independence team: Mary Chapman, Sandra Dennis, Christina Hughes, Jackie Staines and Jan Sunderland.

Cara Acred

Cambridge, January 2013